OF LIFE AND HOPE:
TOWARD EFFECTIVE WITNESS
IN HUMAN RIGHTS

EDITED BY MIA ADJALI

Friendship Press • New York

Dedication

To my parents
Ellen and Hans Aurbakken

Acknowledgments

The following credits express our appreciation to the publishers and writers who have allowed us to use their material in this book.

Preface	From Dwain Epps, in World Council of Churches' document "Human Rights and Christian Responsibility", May 1974.
Chapter 2	Reprinted from *For Their Triumphs and for Their Tears,* by Hilda Bernstein. London: International Defence and Aid Fund, 1975. Used by permission.
Chapter 3	Reprinted from the text of a statement adopted by the World Council of Churches, Geneva, August 1977. Used by permission.
Chapter 6	Reprinted from the text of a statement of the Women's Division, Board of Global Ministries, The United Methodist Church entitled "A Charter for Racial Justice Policies in an Interdependent Global Community", April 1978. Used by permission.
Chapter 7	Reprinted from the text of a statement developed by the Ecumenical Coalition of the Mahoning Valley, Youngstown, Ohio, November 29, 1977. Used by permission.
Chapter 8	Reprinted from the text of a statement issued by the Interfaith Delegation, Montgomery, Alabama, April 19, 1978. Used by permission.
Chapter 9	Reprinted from chapter 5 of *The Children's Political Checklist,* Report #103, September 1977, Early Childhood Project, The Carnegie Foundation on Children, New York City. Used by permission.
Chapter 12	Portions of this chapter are reprinted from two sources: *Food First: Beyond the Myth of Scarcity* by Frances Moore Lappe and Joseph Collins with Cary Fowler, Houghton Mifflin, 1977. *World Hunger: Ten Myths* by Francis Moore Lappe and Joseph Collins. Institute for Food and Development Policy, 1977, revised, 1978. Used by permission.
Chapter 13	Reprinted from "A New Age in Health Care" by R. Nita Barrow. From the February 1978 issue of *response.* Used by permission.
Chapter 15	Reprinted from *Engage/Social Action,* June 1977. c e/sa, as excerpted from a speech by Tom Wicker during an April 1977 Witness Against Executions in Atlanta, Georgia. Used by permission.
Chapter 16	Portions of this chapter are reprinted from two sources: "Why An International Year of the Child? a pamphlet distributed by the U.S. Committee for UNICEF of the United Nations. *Church and Society,* a special issue of the magazine in 1977 entitled "On Being a Child' An Inquiry Into the Needs and Rights of Children and the Commission of the Church." From the foreword by Dr. Thelma Adair. Used by permission.

Untitled poem on page 90 is reprinted from *Adam Among the Television Trees,* © 1971 by Word Incorporated. By permission here of Sandra Ruth Duguid.

Library of Congress Cataloging in Publication Data
Main entry under title:

Of life and hope.

Includes bibliographical references.
    1. Civil rights — Addresses, essays, lectures.
I. Adjali, Mia, 1939-
JC571.037   323.4   79-10324
ISBN 0-377-00084-1

CONTENTS

SECTION I

HUMAN RIGHTS PERTAIN TO INDIVIDUALS AND TO THE HUMAN COLLECTIVES OF WHICH THEY ARE A PART

SECTION II

THE STRUGGLE FOR THE DEFENSE AND PROMOTION OF HUMAN RIGHTS INVOLVES RECOURSE TO POLITICAL ACTION

SECTION III

UNIVERSAL HUMAN RIGHTS APPLY TO OUR OWN SITUATION AS WELL AS TO OTHERS

PREFACE

When I came to see you, brothers, I did not come proclaiming God's secret with any special kind of rhetorical or philosophical brilliance. I had in fact made up my mind that in my preaching to you I would forget everything except Jesus Christ, and him upon his cross....

(1 Cor. 2:1-2, William Barclay)

The biblical accounts of Jesus standing before the rabbis at the age of twelve, organizing a small band of men to raise the consciousness of his people, mixing with the social outcasts, arguing with the rich and the colonial administrators, discussing at length with women, welcoming the children, overturning the tables of the money changers in the temple, riding into Jerusalem at a time when the political climate held danger for a man who dared challenge the authorities of his country—these accounts have always given me a sense of power and freedom. In 1954 my father, Hans Aurbakken, reflecting on Paul's statement in 1 Corinthians, wrote:

> If words could save us we should no longer have to ask the puzzling question about our salvation. Unfortunately, the incredible number of books, sermons, and speeches have failed to answer the one essential question of all times....
>
> Instead of displaying rhetorical or philosophical brilliance Paul chose to think of nothing but a simple fact: Jesus nailed to the cross. An event without beauty, or appealing effect, but whose unique power invades our whole being. For it is by such an action, simple enough to be called simplistic by the world's philosophers, that God decided to save humanity.

Twenty years later Dwain Epps, a staff member of the World Council of Churches, addressing himself to the urgent issue of human rights, echoed a similar reminder. While preparing some documentation for the 1974 World Council of Churches Consultation on Human Rights, Epps wrote:

> A common way to avoid a difficult problem is to remove it from its real context and make of it an abstract discussion subject. Very quickly the causes of the problem are obscured by a haze of words and only the symptoms of it remain visible. The most obvious danger here is that interminable discussions are substituted for effective action. Less obvious is that the fog of abstractions often becomes so thick that we are no longer able to distinguish what is happening to people themselves.[1]

Bearing these thoughts in mind, I should like the following pages to contribute some insight into the nature of the struggles for human rights. These rights were agreed upon by the United Nations when it adopted the Universal Declaration of Human Rights on December 10, 1948.

In 1966 the United Nations adopted and opened for signature and ratification the International Covenant on Civil and Political Rights and the International Covenant on Economic, Social and Cultural Rights. The principles proclaimed in the Declaration were now an integral part of these two legal instruments which, when ratified by a sufficient number of states, would become law. Each covenant is prefaced by the following Preamble:

> The States Parties to the present Covenant,
> Considering that, in accordance with the principles proclaimed in the Charter of the United Nations, recognition of the inherent dignity and of the equal and inalienable rights of all members of the human family is the foundation of freedom, justice and peace in the world,
> *Recognizing* that these rights derive from the inherent dignity of the human person,
> *Recognizing* that, in accordance with the Universal Declaration of Human Rights, the ideal of free human beings enjoying civil and political freedom and freedom from fear and want can only be achieved if conditions are created whereby everyone may enjoy his (her) civil and political rights, as well as his (her) economic, social and cultural rights,
> *Considering* the obligation of States under the Charter of the United Nations to promote universal respect for, and observance of, human rights and freedoms,
> *Realizing* that the individual, having duties to other individuals and to the community to which he (she) belongs, is under a responsibility to strive for the promotion and observance of the rights recognized in the present Covenant,
> *Agree* upon the following articles:...

These Covenants came into force as international legal instruments in 1976 and have become law for those countries which have ratified them. Canada has done so but not the United States. It was not until 1978 that the President, Jimmy Carter, submitted the Covenants to the Senate for ratification.

---

1. Dwain Epps, *Human Rights General Reflection: Three Mistaken Ideas,* WCC-CCIA Document — *Human Rights and Christian Responsibility,* May 1974.

The organization of this study is inspired by the three concepts developed by Dwain Epps in the aforementioned paper.*

Section I: Human rights pertain to individuals and to the human collectives of which they are a part.
Section II: The struggle for the defense and promotion of human rights involves recourse to political action.
Section III: Universal human rights apply to our own situation as well as to others.

Each section is followed by some personal reflections, including suggestions for involving the reader in the movements for human rights. The suggestions constitute some minimal steps necessary for involvement:

Section I: Learning to interpret the signs of the times.
Section II: Agreeing to be part of the struggles.
Section III: Understanding the need for solidarity.

In turn, each section is divided into chapters prefaced by an Article or Articles drawn from the two Human Rights Covenants. One of the objectives of this study is to highlight relevant texts of the Covenants. The content of each chapter, however, is not a treatise or legal discussion on the meaning of the right or rights. Instead, it focuses on what is happening to people and describes their involvement in defending or promoting rights. As Christians our focus should always be on "what is happening to people" and acting toward each other—and others—as God acts toward us.

> Christ calls us to a life of love. In love there are no rights, for love is a gift, freely given. It is only little by little, however, that we learn to love. Thus the concept of rights becomes helpful as a step toward an ideal human order....As expressed in the UN Covenants, then, rights are not an end in themselves; rather they are one of the necessary means toward a rich human climate in which we can learn to truly love one another in full human freedom.
>
> Mary Litell in Chapter 17 of this book

Throughout biblical history the people of God have had opportunities to express and act in human terms a measure of God's love. "God has told you what is good; and what is it that the Lord asks of you? Only to act justly, to love loyalty, to walk wisely before your God " (Micah 6:8).

This study assumes our willingness to draw strength from our faith and understanding of God's action in history. "I will recount the Lord's acts of unfailing love and the Lord's praises as High God, all that the Lord has done for us and his great goodness to the house of Israel, all that he has done for them in his tenderness and by his many acts of love" (Isaiah 63:7). As Christians we should be able to face many critical situations in our world believing God's "unfailing love" and, together with people of other faiths and other beliefs, struggle for life, hope and human dignity, creating the conditions which will bring that "rich human climate in which we can learn to truly love one another in full human freedom."

---

*The intent of the article is maintained; emphasis and language have been slightly altered with the author's permission.

SECTION I

HUMAN RIGHTS PERTAIN TO INDIVIDUALS AND TO THE HUMAN COLLECTIVES OF WHICH THEY ARE A PART

INTRODUCTION

It is often said that human rights pertain only to individuals and are not applicable to the human collectives of which they are part. It was the view of eighteenth and nineteenth century liberalism that society is but an agglomeration of individuals who must be protected from the social restrictions to their full and free human development.

Some churches, bound up with a theology that stressed individual salvation, have often reinforced this idea, considering the secular world to be a sort of prison from which the human spirit must be freed. Today this traditional theology has given way to an affirmation that the Christian must be concerned for the whole person whose social relations complement rather than detract from his/her humanity. We understand the gospel to call individuals into the whole— there to be instruments of humanization, liberation, and change. The serious question facing the churches is how to manifest actively their concern for individuals who are integral parts of a larger society. Clearly, no simplistic approach such as the individualistic one will permit effective action in societies that are increasingly complex.

Looking beneath the surface of contemporary talk about individual freedoms, we see the stark truth that the vast majority of violations of individuals' human rights come as a result of their belonging to a certain sector of society.

Dwain Epps

1

CHAPTER 1
SELF-DETERMINATION
DONALD WILL

Article 1

1. All peoples have the *right of self-determination*. By virtue of that right they freely determine their political status and freely pursue their economic, social and cultural development.

2. All peoples may, for their own ends, freely dispose of their natural wealth and resources without prejudice to any obligations arising out of international economic co-operation, based upon the principle of mutual benefit, and international law. *In no case may a people be deprived of its own means of subsistence.*

3. The States Parties to the present Covenant, including those having responsibility for the administration on Non-Self-Governing and Trust Territories, shall promote the realization of the right of self-determination, and shall respect that right, in conformity with the provisions of the Charter of the United Nations.

International Covenant on Civil and
Political Rights, and
International Covenant on Economic,
Social and Cultural Rights (Italics added)

"All peoples have the right of self-determination. By virtue of this right they freely determine their political status and freely pursue their economic, social and cultural development." This statement constitutes Part I, Article I, of both the International Covenant on Civil and Political Rights and the International Covenant on Economic, Social and Cultural Rights. Indeed, the right of self-determination is one of the most basic rights of all peoples. Deprivation of a people's right to self-determination very often is the root cause of other forms of human rights violations against them.

The criteria which define a "people" and which distinguish them from other peoples are a complex and highly subjective matter. Generally accepted grounds would include a common language, culture, historical experience, and residence in a proximate area. When one of these factors is lacking, strong communality in the others may lead persons to identify themselves as a people. This act of self-identification itself is important as it reflects their desire to share a common future.

As indicated in the Covenants, the right to self-determination has two aspects: the determination of political status and the pursuit of economic, social and cultural development. In determining their political status, a people may opt for one of several different alternatives. They may choose to constitute themselves as an independent nation, or they may opt for a confederation with another people, or perhaps autonomy within a larger nation. The choice primarily depends upon the particular history of the people in question and their relations with other people near or among whom they live.

One of the key factors related to self-determination is land. For a people to exercise political, economic, social and cultural rights, they must be able to exercise them in a given area. Often the expropriation of a people's land is one of the manifestations of the denial of their right to self-determination.

Donald Will is presently working on his Ph.D. in International Relations from the University of Denver. He has published articles on the Middle East and the New International Economic Order. He has been in the Middle East twice since 1975.

Realization of the right to self-determination generally involves a long arduous struggle. This struggle may at times even include armed struggle (as the American Revolution itself did). The political questions which arise during the struggle are manifold. They include the specific delineation of the goals of the struggle, the achievement of international recognition, and relations with the power(s) denying the rights being sought. As with the question of political status, each people will resolve the matters according to the particular characteristics of their situation.

The political aspects of human rights are often most evident; yet the economic, social and cultural factors are just as important for the survival of a people. These factors are inextricably interwoven in the right to self-determination.

If people are deprived of the right to determine under what form of government they wish to live, this may lead to an inability to control their economy, pursue their social goals, or preserve their culture. They may even be deliberately prevented from exercising their political right to self-determination because it would allow them to resist or throw off external exploitation of their economic resources.

Likewise a people might be deprived of the right of cultural self-determination in order to obscure the fact of their economic or political oppression. For instance, in the case of the French-speaking people of Quebec—the Quebecois—denials of cultural freedom such as use of French in the national media and schools have helped obscure their common identity and the economic oppression which they have suffered as a people (e.g., an unemployment rate twice that of English-speaking Canadians). The right of self-determination is, therefore, best examined in its entirety.

A sense of what self-determination means, and how people may go about expressing it, may be gained by examining three peoples' struggles for self-determination. Each of these is of significant relevance to North Americans. The three peoples are the Palestinians, the Native Americans, and the Puerto Ricans. In so short a piece as this, it is obviously impossible to do justice to the complexity of each of these issues. The cursory descriptions which follow are presented to convey what self-determination means and what the recognition of this right implies for North Americans.

Palestinian Self-Determination

The creation of the state of Israel in 1948 resulted in over half the Arab population of Palestine becoming refugees. Another 300,000 Palestinians were displaced as a result of the 1967 War. With the natural population increase, this brings the present refugee population to 1.8 million. About half a million Palestinians reside in Israel, while approximately 1.5 million live under Israeli occupation in the West Bank and Gaza Strip. The right of the Palestinian people to return to their homes has been repeatedly endorsed by the United Nations. General Assembly Resolution No. 3236 of November 22, 1974, "*Reaffirms* the inalienable rights of the Palestinian people in Palestine, including: (a) The right to self-determination without external interference; (b) The right to national independence and sovereignty."

In the course of struggles for self-determination, popular movements develop which express the goals of the people. In the case of the Palestinian people, the Palestine Liberation Organization not only carries out the political and military aspects of their cause, but also provides social services and cultural cohesion. The political program of the Palestine Liberation Organization reflects their assessment of how best to achieve self-determination in their land. At present this program calls for the establishment of a Palestinian political entity or state on any part of Palestine which they liberate. Coupled with the return of refugees, this state would allow the Palestinian people to struggle alongside progressive Israelis for the creation of a democratic state in the whole of Palestine. At this stage of the struggle, non-military means would take precedence.

For North Americans the right of Palestinian self-determination is very important. Many Jews and Arabs in Canada and the United States (citizens and non-citizens alike) are committed to one side or the other of the issue. In the United States everyone is involved at least indirectly through the foreign policy of the United States which places major emphasis on the Israeli-Palestinian conflict. This is reflected by the staggering amount of armaments the United States has transferred to the region.

Although the Carter administration acknowledged that Palestinians have "rights," the United States has yet to recognize the right of the Palestinians to a state of their own. The fact that the United States has not done so contributes to the ongoing suffering of the Palestinians in refugee camps as well as to the volatility of a conflict which threatens the peace of the whole world. As of the writing of this piece, Israel and Egypt are involved in negotiations growing out of the Camp David Summit. The present agreement does not make provision for full Palestinian self-determination and has been soundly condemned by both the Palestine Liberation Organization and the majority of political notables in the Occupied Territories.

Native American Self-Determination

When Europeans first arrived in the Americas, they found both continents populated by the peoples whom they mistakenly called Indians. In what is now the United States these peoples formed about three hundred different nations with estimates of the total population being as high as thirty million. The fact that less than one million native people presently live in the United States tells the story of the brutal oppression received at the hands of the European colonists and the United States government which they created. Genocide, though, is only a part of the history of Native Americans. Despite the fact that the Native Americans received them cordially, the colonists soon set about seizing the land, disrupting the environment, destroying the economy, and alternately restricting and demeaning the culture of the native peoples. The Native Americans put up a strong resistance but were outgunned and soon outnumbered. It is a bitter irony that their struggle for survival has received world renown through the racist distortions of that Hollywood creation—the American western. These movies have sought to justify or excuse the oppression of Native Americans in both a crude ("the dishonest Indian") and a sophisticated ("the unavoidable result of modernization") fashion.

Although much of their land was simply seized, in some cases the Native Americans signed treaties with the colonists and later with the United States government regarding land ownership (a concept alien to them to begin with). These treaties were progressively broken over the years, whittling away at the land controlled by the native peoples. Today those Native Americans not wishing to assimilate are confronted with a reservation system controlled by the United States government.

The American Indian Movement, founded in 1968, has emerged as the leading group in the Native American struggle for self-determination. Their activities include the creation of survival schools in which Indian children are taught according to their own customs and traditions. Political actions range from direct resistance, such as the Wounded Knee Occupation, to the creation of the International Indian Treaty Council which raises the native peoples' cause at the United Nations.

The basic political demands of the American Indian Movement regarding self-determination are:

1) That the United States honor all treaties made with Indian Nations;

2) That the United States repeal the Indian Reorganization Act [which created puppet governments on the reservations] and allow Indian Nations to set up their own forms of government;

3) That the United States government remove the Bureau of Indian Affairs from the Department of the Interior and turn it over to the control of Indian people.

The right of Native Americans to control their own land has been opposed in a great part because United States corporations, through the collusion of the Bureau of Indian Affairs, are profiting from the resources of the Indian lands. The impact of the Alaskan pipeline on Native American land use and lifestyle is a recent and blatant evidence of this. Also, for the United States to recognize the sovereignty of Native Americans is to implicitly admit the crimes perpetrated against them over several hundred years.

Puerto Rican Self-Determination

Spanish colonization of Puerto Rico began with Christopher Columbus's arrival there in 1493 and the conquering of the island by Juan Ponce de Leon in 1508. The Spanish enslaved the native peoples of Boriquen (which they later renamed Puerto Rico) and treated them brutally. Within three years the Indians had been driven to rebellion. By the middle of the 1500s thousands of the native people of Puerto Rico had been killed or died of disease under Spanish oppression. In 1526 Charles V, the king of Spain, acknowledged the horrible treatment of the Indians by the Spanish settlers and commanded that thereafter they be treated as free men and women. To replace the forced labor thus lost to them, the settlers began importing African slaves. By 1800 "native people," the Africans, and the Spanish had begun to fuse into a distinct people with its own culture. The independence movement sweeping the Americas during the 1800s culminated in Puerto Rico with the "Grito de Lares" on September 23, 1868, when nationalists captured the town of Lares and declared Puerto Rico a Republic. Bloodily crushed by the Spanish, this uprising is still celebrated today in Puerto Rico. During the Spanish-American War of 1898 the United States seized several Spanish colonies including the Philippines, Cuba, and Puerto Rico. Unlike the first two, Puerto Rico never gained its independence.

Puerto Rico presently has Commonwealth status

with the United States. Some Puerto Ricans favor the continuation of this status, others favor statehood for Puerto Rico, while still others favor independence. In the last election the party favoring statehood received the largest vote. Some of the parties advocating independence had called for a boycott of the election. The pro-independence parties have been the object of political harassment by the United States authorities. For a vote or plebiscite to be truly representative, these groups would have to enjoy the unhindered right to organize.

Concentration on the political questions, however, tends to neglect the economic aspects of Puerto Rican self-determination. Approximately two million people, about 40 percent of the people of Puerto Rican origin, live today in the United States. A primary reason for their departure from Puerto Rico is lack of jobs. Unemployment on the island is high and the economy is dominated by United States corporations. Puerto Ricans have little ability to determine the course of their own economy.

For North Americans it is crucial to recognize the right of Puerto Ricans to control their own political and economic destiny. The United States government and corporate interests should acknowledge the right of Puerto Ricans who advocate independence to organize around that cause. North Americans also need to be aware of inadequate or slanted media coverage which often ignores the pro-independence parties.

Indeed, on December 14, 1973, the report of the United Nations Special Committee on Decolonization was approved by the General Assembly by a vote of 105 to 5 with 10 abstentions. The report reaffirmed "...the inalienable right of the people of Puerto Rico to self-determination and independence..." and called on the government of the United States "...to refrain from taking any measures which might obstruct the full and free exercise..." of those rights.

As the preceding examples should make apparent, securing the right of self-determination for all peoples will be a long, hard struggle. Those striving to gain their rights must decide what political-economic structures will best allow for their self-determination. Then they must find what course of action will best bring about their goals. Those North Americans among us who find these efforts to achieve self-determination threatening to our own interests must struggle with that issue. We should try to break through the economic and cultural barriers which divide us all and try to understand why self-determination may be necessary for the survival of peoples such as the Native Americans, Palestinians or Puerto Ricans.

Self-determination is a human right. As with all human rights and freedoms, it cannot be truly enjoyed at the expense of the rights of others. Those of us who have the right to self-determination should act to assure that our own government, economy, and culture do not infringe upon the political, economic, social or cultural rights of others. This is especially true if we are standing in the way of another people's struggle for self-determination.

Questions for Reflection

1. What is the relationship between political and economic self-determination? Can one be achieved in the absence of the other?

2. What are some of the problems of exercising cultural self-determination in a society dominated by another culture? It will be useful to reflect on some of the particular problems which Native Americans have in this regard.

3. What similarities and differences exist between Native American quests for self-determination and those of other peoples?

4. What political and historical factors lead some groups to resort to armed struggle to achieve self-determination, while others do not?

5. For what reasons have the governments of the United States and Canada often been in conflict with movements for self-determination? What can concerned citizens do about this?

6. Why does denial of the right of self-determination usually lead to the denial of other human rights?

Exercises for Reflection

1. In Chapter 12, "To Ensure Availability of Food for All," read the last point of the "Ten Food Self-Reliance Fundamentals." Note that it redefines what we can do to *help* those in the world suffering from hunger: "Work to remove those obstacles preventing people from taking charge of their food-producing resources—obstacles that today are being built by our government, by U.S.-supported international agencies and U.S.-based corporations." Relate the struggle for self-determination to the struggle for "food self-determination" as discussed in that chapter. Some questions to consider are: (a) Is it necessary to be free from hunger to enjoy political rights? (b) Why has the achievement of self-determination by most North Americans not ensured freedom from hunger for all persons living in North America? (c) Why are hunger and economic deprivation more prevalent among

those peoples in North America who are denied self-determination?

2. In the Preface to Section I, Dwain Epps raises the relation between individual rights and collective rights. He concludes by stating that "...the vast majority of violations of individuals' human rights come as a result of their belonging to a certain sector of society." Relate individual rights to the collective right of self-determination. What are some of the individual rights violations which may stem from the denial of the right of self-determination? How might they arise?

3. In *Paradox and Promise in Human Rights,* Peggy Billings suggests (Chapter 2, p.39) that as a justice of the International Court of Justice you hear the cases of Antonio Millape, Mapuche Confederation vs. the Government of Chile, and Ed Bernstick, Cree Nation vs. the Government of Canada. What would be your verdict?

4. Those in your community or church engaged in a study on the Middle East could give additional input to your questions relating to this chapter.

Preparing for Effective Witness: Further Reading

"Something New," Chapter 2, pp. 32-55, and Chapter 4, "The Case of the Indigenous Peoples of the Americas," pp. 86-95, in *Paradox and Promise in Human Rights* by Peggy Billings (New York: Friendship Press, 1979).

"The Exploitation of the Covenant," Chapter 10, pp. 67-74, in *The Liberating Bond: Covenants—Biblical and Contemporary* by Wolfgang Roth and Rosemary Radford Ruether (New York: Friendship Press, 1978).

Resources

On the Palestinian People:

Peace in the Middle East? by Noam Chomsky (New York: Vintage, 1974). A good overall analysis of the Israeli-Palestinian conflict.

Our Roots Are Still Alive by People's Press, P. O. Box 40130, San Francisco, California 94110. A history of the displacement and struggle of the Palestinian people.

Palestine Human Rights Bulletin, 1322 18th Street, N.W., Washington, D.C. 20036.

Where We Stand—Statements of American Churches on the Middle East Conflict, Middle East Peace Project, 339 Lafayette, New York, New York 10012. A compilation of current position statements and resolutions by churches in the United States.

Peace, Justice and Reconciliation in the Arab-Israeli Conflict: A Christian Perspective. Resulting in work done by a study group established by the Ecumenical Forum of Canada. Published in 1979. Available from Friendship Press.

"The Key," a 30-minute color film made for the UN Conference on the Habitat describing the living conditions of the Palestinian people and their struggle to return home. Available from Palestine Information Office, 1326 18th Street, N.W., Washington, D.C. 20036.

"To Live in Freedom," a one-hour film on the Israeli-Palestinian conflict made by Israeli dissidents. Available from Third World Newsreel, 160 Fifth Avenue, New York, New York 10010 and California Newsreel, 630 Natoma, San Francisco, CA 94103.

On the Native American People:
The following can be obtained from American Indian Treaty Council Information Center, 870 Market Street, San Francisco, California 94102:

• *The Great Sioux Nation* by Roxanne Dunbar Ortiz. Contains an oral history of the Sioux nation and its struggle for sovereignty.

• *The Geneva Conference.* Official report by the International Indian Treaty Council on the International Non-Governmental Organization Conference on Discrimination Against Indigenous Populations — 1977 — In the Americas, September 20-23.

• *Treaty Council News.* Official Bulletin of the International Indian Treaty Council.

"We Are the Evidence of This Western Hemisphere." Videotape documenting the Second International Indian Treaty Conference, 1976. Explains the history, struggles and goals of those involved in Indian movements for self-determination and sovereignty.

"The Question That You Should Ask," a 35-minute slide show on the Native American struggle. Available from the Native American Solidarity Committee, P.O. Box 3426, St. Paul, Minnesota 55165.

Sovereignty and Jurisdiction, a 1976 special issue of the American Indian Journal published by the Institute for the Development of Indian Law, Inc., Suite 200, 925 15th Street, N.W., Washington, D.C. 20005.

"Mohawk Nation," a 45-minute documentary dealing with Indian treaty rights and focusing specifically on the Mohawks' seizing of abandoned land in New York State as part of their ancestral homeland. The film shows the Mohawk re-establishing their traditional way of life and imparting this to their children. Available from Third World Newsreel, 160 Fifth Avenue, Room 911, New York, New York 10010. Rental: $75. Sale: $600.

Akwesasne Notes, c/o Mohawk Nation, Roosevel-town, New York 13683.

On the Puerto Rican people:

Puerto Rico: A People Challenging Colonialism, EPICA Task Force, 1500 Farragut Square, N.W., Washington,D.C. 20011. An introduction to the Puerto Rican people's struggle by Ecumenical Program for Interamerican Communication and Action (EPICA).

Puerto Rico, Si! Fact sheets on the Colonial Domination of Puerto Rico by the Committee for Puerto Rican Decolonization, Box 1240, Peter Stuyvesant Station, New York, New York 10009.

Puerto Rico Libre! Bulletin of the Puerto Rican Solidarity Committee, Box 319, Cooper Station, New York, New York 10003.

"Introduction to Puerto Rico," a factual look at the historical and contemporary situation of Puerto Rico: history and cultural identity, international relations, social studies, immigration, and the geographical importance of the island in both the Latin American and Caribbean contexts. Two parts of 15 minutes each. Available from Latin American Film Project, P.O. Box 315, Franklin Lakes, New Jersey 07417.

"Puerto Rico: Paradise Invaded," shows representative individualized voices which characterize the persistent hopes and aspirations of the Puerto Rican people. Includes the contemporary relationship between Puerto Rico and the U.S.; the imposition of short-term economic changes which cause the demographic and cultural disintegration of Puerto Rican national identity; the economic exile: life in New York; and environmental pollution of the island. 30 minutes. Available from Latin American Film Project, P.O. Box 315, Franklin Lakes, New Jersey 07417.

Organizations to contact for further information
Palestine Information Office
1326 18th Street, N.W.
Washington,D.C. 20036

Palestine Human Rights Campaign
1322 18th Street, N.W.
Washington, D.C. 20036

International Indian Treaty Council
870 Market Street
San Francisco, California 94102

Native American Solidarity Committee
P.O. Box 3426
St. Paul, Minnesota 55165

Ecumenical Program for Interamerican Communication & Action (EPICA)
1500 Farragut Square, N.W.
Washington, D.C. 20011

North American Congress on Latin America (NACLA)
Box 57, Cathedral Station
New York, New York 10025

Committee on Decolonization
United Nations
New York, New York 10017

Committee on the Inalienable Rights of the Palestinian People
United Nations
New York, New York 10017

Inter-Church Committee on Human Rights in Latin America
40 St. Clair Avenue
E. Toronto, Ontario M7A, 1T7

CHAPTER 2
MIGRANT LABOUR -
THE BREAKING OF FAMILIES *
HILDA BERNSTEIN

Article 8

1. No one shall be *held in slavery;* slavery and the slave-trade in all their forms shall be prohibited.

2. No one shall be *held in servitude.*

3. (a) No one shall be required to perform *forced or compulsory labour;*

   (b) Paragraph 3 *(a)* shall not be held to preclude, in countries where imprisonment with hard labour may be imposed as a punishment for a crime, the performance of hard labour in pursuance of a sentence to such punishment by a competent court;

   (c) For the purpose of this paragraph the term "forced or compulsory labour" shall not include:

   (i) Any work or service, not referred to in sub-paragraph *(b),* normally required of a person who is under detention in consequence of a lawful order of a court, or of a person during conditional release from such detention;

   (ii) Any service of a military character and, in countries where conscientious objection is recognized, any national service required by law of conscientious objectors;

   (iii) Any service exacted in cases of emergency or calamity threatening the life or well-being of the community;

   (iv) Any work or service which forms part of normal civil obligations.

International Covenant on Civil and Political Rights (Italics added)

Editor's Note

One of the interdenominational mission study themes in 1976-77 was "The Nations of Southern Africa: Dilemma for Christians." The following analysis comes from *Adult-Youth Guide on "The Nations of Southern Africa"* by John Stevens Kerr and is useful to understand the paper which follows.

South Africa: Situational Analysis

1) This is one of the richest, most industrialized nations in the world. Total population is nearly 25 million—slightly more than Canada's. Of these, about 4.2 million (17 percent) are white. They control the political and economic life of the 17,740,000 native Africans, 2,330,000 "coloureds" (mixed blood), and 700,000 Asians.

2) **South Africa is devoted to apartheid, a policy of separating the races. Eighty-seven percent of the total land has been reserved for whites only. The remaining 13 percent of the land is divided into 100 separate sections called bantustans (homelands). In these bantustans the black population will live, divided by tribal affiliation. All principal towns, mineral resources, and industry are in the white areas, together with most of the productive farmland.**

3) **Because the white economy needs cheap labor—and by law blacks can be paid only a fraction of prevailing white wages—some blacks receive special permission to work in white areas. Those who do must have permits, live in special ghettos, and regularly report to labor officials who keep track of their whereabouts through computers. About 8 million blacks now work under this system in white areas.**

4) **The government says "black workers must not be burdened with superfluous appendages like women and children." About one-half of the workers must leave their families behind in the bantustan, seeing their wives and children one month out of the year.**

5) **Bantustans, according to official estimates, can support only 2.5 million persons at a subsistence level. Some 7 million have now been moved to these areas. Disease and death run rampant. The government hopes to locate industry right outside the bantustans, but so far this policy has not met with much success.**

6) **Under "Master and Servant Laws," a black working outside the bantustan has no rights. He or she can be jailed for absenteeism, refusing to obey a foreman's order or for changing jobs. Black unions and most strikes are illegal. A black gold miner receives $9.60 per week, while his white counterpart earns about $150 per week.[1]**

To achieve its primary position of wealth, strength and power, South Africa has drawn on and required a constant supply of cheap black labour.

Postwar Europe is familiar with the phenomenon of migrant workers leaving their own country to work in another for a specified period. There are such migrant workers in South Africa as well, 367,000 of them who come from other African states to work in the mines, leaving their families in their own countries and ultimately returning to them. These fall outside the scope of this book, which is confined to the internal migrant.

In the distorting mirror of apartheid, all black workers outside the reserves are migrants who leave their own "country" to work in white South Africa—a different country. This precept is now being applied not merely to those workers from rural areas who seek employment in the towns, but also to those settled communities of black families who have often been town-dwellers for two or three generations.

Migrant labour, as other communities have found to their cost, has an adverse effect on family life and social development, as the men who should be playing their part as husbands, fathers, and members of the community are absent for long periods. Where such dislocation is temporary and small-scale the effects may be remedied but in South Africa the intention is to turn the entire black work force into migrant labour—permanently.

There are still in existence large black townships serving the towns and industries, notably Soweto outside Johannesburg, where workers live with their wives and young children. But in other such townships—Alexandra, also outside Johannesburg—all family housing has been destroyed, wives, children, and old people despatched to "resettlement" camps in the reserves, and hostels provided for "single" black workers. "We are trying to introduce the migratory

Hilda Bernstein is a South African writer who has played an active role in the liberation movement and is now in exile. Her previous books for International Defense and Aid Fund for Southern Africa include *No. 46—Steve Biko*.

*Reprinted from Chapter 2 of *For Their Triumphs and For Their Tears: Women in Apartheid South Africa* by Hilda Bernstein (London: International Defense and Aid Fund, 1975).

1. John Stevens Kerr, *Adult-Youth Guide on "The Nations of Southern Africa"* (New York: Friendship Press, 1976), p.11.

labour pattern as far as possible in every sphere," stated a prominent Nationalist MP, Mr. G. F. van L. Froneman, who later became Deputy Minister of Justice, Mines and Planning. "This is, in fact, the entire basis of our policy as far as the white economy is concerned."[2]

It is estimated today that half of the African labour force in the urban areas are migrants. They are not seasonal labourers, but part of the grand design of apartheid by which the inherent contradiction between an ideological theory demanding race separation, and the needs of a developed industrialized economy requiring a constant supply of cheap labour can be reconciled.

Migrant labour causes the destruction of family life and turns human beings into units of labour to be manipulated at will, while wives and children become unnecessary dependents who must be removed from the urban areas where they serve no purpose for the white economy.

In 1969 Mr. Froneman named the conditions under which "foreign labour" (that is, South African blacks) could be used without conflicting with apartheid. Among them: no rights of domicile or citizenship in the white homeland. And "This African labour force must not be burdened with superfluous appendages such as wives, children and dependents who could not provide service."[3]

"We need them to work for us," stated the Prime Minister, Mr. B. J. Vorster, "but the fact that they work for us can never entitle them to claim political rights. Not now, nor in the future...under any circumstances."[4]

"It is accepted Government policy that Bantu are only temporarily resident in European areas as long as they offer labour," said an official circular from the Department of Bantu Administration (12 December 1967). "Bantu in European areas who are normally regarded as non-productive and have to be resettled in the homeland areas are: (a) the aged, the unfit, women with dependent children, squatters on mission stations, etc; (b) professional Bantu such as doctors, attorneys, industrialists."

The official term, "temporary sojourners," is applied to African workers who are integrated with, and (are) an integral part of the country's economy. They are allowed to work in that economy because it would collapse without them. But they are not regarded as human beings. A resolution passed at the 1973 Congress of the Afrikaanse Studentebond (Afrikaner students' organisation) demanded that "All the black women and children in the white area be shipped back to the homelands and only the men should be left in the white areas for as long as we need them."

Other aspects of the official view are no less inhuman. "We do not want the Bantu women here simply as an adjunct to the procreative capacity of the Bantu population."[5] A wife should be allowed into the town only if she were needed on the labour market. Her husband could visit her from time to time.

This official concept of family life for the blacks—where husband and wife normally live apart but the husband may sometimes visit his wife—is underlined in a circular from the Department of Bantu Administration and Development to local authorities in 1969. The circular put forward the proposition that where a (white) town is close to a "homeland," the Africans employed in that town should actually live in the "homeland." Should the distance between town and "homeland" be too great, however, hostel accommodation should be provided for the workers in the urban areas, who should be able to visit their families periodically.

When the Black Sash wrote to all South African churches stating that since the church preached the sanctity of marriage and family life, they should protest against official policy, the largest of the Christian Churches, the Nederduits Gereformeerde Kerk (Dutch Reformed Church) replied, "That families in many cases cannot live together is true but it is also true that they are granted the opportunity to visit each other—provided of course they are willing to comply with the relevant regulations and they do not disregard this privilege."[6]

In *Migrant Labour in South Africa,* Francis Wilson says that the migrant labour system is based on the premise that a human being can be broken into two parts: a "labour unit" working in town, separated from the other part, a man with a family, with hopes and aspirations. "If man was seen primarily as a human being who among other things was a worker, then such exclusion would not be possible."[7]

In the special language of apartheid, blacks are not ordinary human beings. They are labour units, who are productive or non-productive; who are temporary sojourners in the towns even though they may spend their whole lives working there; or illegal immigrants

2. House of Assembly Debates, 6-2-68.
3. Debates, 23-5-69.
4. Debates, 24-4-68.

5. Debates, 17-3-64.
6. Black Sash, 1974.
7. Francis Wilson, *Migrant Labour in South Africa* (Johannesburg, 1972).

within the borders of their own country, whose wives and children are superfluous appendages—non-productive, the women being nothing more than adjuncts to the procreative capacity of the black male labour unit. Only through this process of de-humanisation is the application of inhuman laws possible.

Migrant labour exerts a powerful force on the lives of South African women. The system itself makes it virtually illegal for the majority of African women to live with their husbands, except during the annual two-week holiday when migrant workers may go to visit their wives in the reserves. It makes a mockery of family life, cutting an impassable chasm between husband and wife.

Official statistics about the marital status of South African women of various races tell their own story about the social consequences of the migrant labour system. According to the results of the 1970 census there were more married white females (843,000) than there were unmarried (837,940). Married white women as a proportion of all white females (1,870,360—including widows, divorcees, etc.) constituted 45 percent of the total. In contrast, amongst Africans, married women (2,153,860) constituted only 28.2 percent of all females (7,649,020), and were less than half as numerous as those who were unmarried (4,740,300).

Migrant labour is the most important single factor in the life of South Africa, affecting the lives of every single person living in the reserves, a large proportion of all workers in urban areas, and indirectly the lives of all South Africans, black and white. During the long periods of their youthful, sexually active lives, husbands and wives must live apart. For many, a family unit is never formed. The result is social chaos.

Francis Wilson sums up the evidence of his research on migrant labour with a devastating list of 31 arguments against it, including many that touch directly on the lives of women. Among others, it aggravates and creates illegitimacy, bigamy and prostitution; homosexuality and drunkenness; breakdown of parental authority; malnutrition, tuberculosis and venereal disease. Together with influx control and mass removals under "resettlement" plans, migrant labour is depriving millions of black women of the most elementary and fundamental rights, and creating the conditions for untold tragedies.

Questions for Reflection

1. According to this description of African labour in South Africa, is it justified to suggest this is "servitude" or "forced or compulsory labour" (Article 8 of the International Covenant on Civil and Political Rights)? In what way?

2. In the International Covenant on Economic, Social and Cultural Rights, Articles 6 & 7 (see Chapter 7) the States not only recognize the "right to work" in a job freely chosen, but the right to "enjoyment of just and favourable conditions of work" which includes "decent living" for the workers and their families. How does South Africa live up to these standards according to this presentation?

3. What effects do South Africa's labour policies have on African families? Look at Chapter 9, "To Promote the General Welfare." What role do you feel the government should take to protect the family as "the natural and fundamental group unit of society"?

Exercises for Reflection

1. Discuss the premise that a human being can be broken into two parts, "a labor unit" and "a man with a family." Relate this assumption to the Christian's understanding that a man and a woman are made in God's image—and to the commandment "Love your neighbor as yourself."

2. What changes have occurred in South Africa since Pieter Botha was elected Prime Minister in 1978? What effect has he had on the labor policies of South Africa? Describe life for Africans today. Discuss the options the Africans have for making changes in their country. What role do you think the Church should play in a situation like that? What can Christians in the United States and Canada do to help correct abuses in South Africa? (For this exercise it will be important to gather clippings from newspapers describing the situation in South Africa. Some useful resources are also listed.)

3. Perhaps the most important violation of human rights in South Africa is the right of self-determination as raised in Chapter 1. Do the Africans "determine their political status and freely pursue their economic and social and cultural development"? Relate this chapter to questions in Chapter 1 and to the Preface to Section I.

Preparing for Effective Witness: Further Reading

"To Restore the Economic Health of the Community," Chapter 7 (in this book).

"To Secure a Correction of Abuses," Chapter 8.

"To Promote the General Welfare," Chapter 9.

Resources

For Their Triumphs and For Their Tears: Women in Apartheid South Africa by Hilda Bernstein (London:

International Defense and Aid Fund, 1975). Available from International Defense and Aid Fund for Southern Africa, P.O. Box 17, Cambridge, Mass. 02138.

African Workers and Apartheid by David Davis. Fact Paper on Southern Africa #5, International Defense and Aid Fund, London, 1978. Available from same address as above.

Apartheid in Practice, No. OPI/553, United Nations. Available from Sales Section, Room A-3315, United Nations, New York, New York 10017. Cost: 75 cents.

Objective Justice, a quarterly review, published by the United Nations Office of Public Information, covering United Nations activities for the self-determination of peoples, the elimination of racial discrimination and apartheid, and the advancement of human rights. Single issues may be obtained for $1.00 by writing to: United Nations Publications, Room A-3315, New York, New York 10017. Subscriptions: $3.00 for one year.

Torment to Triumph in Southern Africa by Louise Stack and Don Morton, and the *Adult-Youth Guide on "The Nations of Southern Africa"* by John Stevens Kerr, were both used in the 1976-77 Interdenominational Mission Study on the theme "The Nations of Southern Africa: Dilemma for Christians." Available from Friendship Press, 475 Riverside Drive, New York, New York 10027.

Audio-visuals

"The Beloved Country Cries: The Church and Apartheid." Amid the racial tensions and oppression occasioned by the system of apartheid in South Africa, what role can the church play? Bishop Desmond Tutu, Episcopal leader in Lesotho, outlines with correspondent Bill Matney problems and opportunities for his people. Black & white, 30 minutes. Available from TV Film Library, Room 860, 475 Riverside Drive, New York, N.Y. 10027. Rental: $12.

"Last Grave at Dimbaza," a documentary on the effects of apartheid in South Africa from the black viewpoint. Depicts attitudes of Afrikaners and white South Africans who feel that the country is theirs, and the system of oppression maintained by brutal control. 55 minutes. Write for rental information to CC Films, Room 860, 475 Riverside Drive, New York, N.Y. 10027. Sale: $425 (to religious groups only).

"Rising Tide." Under apartheid, Africans have no rights. The film describes the differences between life in South Africa for the Europeans and for the Africans. The film focuses on the relationships of South Africa to Zimbabwe, to Namibia, and to Angola. The film describes the role of multinationals in South Africa—South Africa's foreign trade, its arms buildup, and its role at the UN. The intensity of African protest since 1976 is vividly portrayed. The soundtrack has numerous interviews with African leaders and with people in the streets, nationalistic songs, and a commentary. Available from Southern Africa Media Center, 630 Natoma, San Francisco, California 94103 and from Icarus Films, Inc., 200 Park Ave. South, Room 1319, New York, New York 10003. Write for rental information.

"South Africa: Freedom Rising" is a collection of photographs on slides from the inside of South Africa, set to African "freedom music" and narration, to show the history and everyday experience of apartheid. The how and why of apartheid are explained. The audience sees the fundamental role it plays in South African economy, its effect in the United States, and some things that can be done about it. Slide-tape available from Dayton Community Media Workshop, 215 Superior Avenue, Dayton, Ohio 45406. Rental: $20. Sale: $75.

"South Africa—the White Laager" traces the history of the Afrikaans from the 1800s to the present (1976), giving a factual understanding of the political and social structure of past and present South Africa. Contains interviews with many elements of society, points out the injustices of the government, and discusses the lack of human rights. 58 minutes. Available from N.Y.U. Film Library, 26 Washington Place, New York, New York 10003. Rental: $40.

Organizations to contact for further information

Toronto Committee for the Liberation of Southern Africa (TCLSAC)
121 Avenue Road
Toronto, Ontario

American Committee on Africa
198 Broadway
New York, New York 10038

Washington Office on Africa
110 Maryland Avenue, N.E.
Washington, D.C. 20002

South Africa Freedom Committee (SAFCO)
310 East 44th Street, Rm. 1703
New York, New York 10017

Centre Against Apartheid
United Nations
New York, New York 10017

CHAPTER 3
TORTURE
STATEMENT BY THE WORLD COUNCIL OF CHURCHES

Article 7

No one shall be subjected to *torture or to cruel, inhuman or degrading treatment or punishment*. In particular, no one shall be subjected without his (her) free consent to medical or scientific experimentation.

International Covenant on Civil and Political Rights (Italics added)

Human beings will rebel against depersonalization. The new localism is such a rebellion. The only question is whether it will be positive or negative in the form it takes. The widespread and unabashed use of torture is evidence that we may have reached the ultimate stage of depersonalization in a technological world. People have been torturing other people throughout all of history, but in this century we have arrived at international consensus that this practice is wrong and not to be tolerated by any self-respecting person or group. Any other position is untenable. The claim of human rights may be a slender reed, but it is our defense against the savage in ourselves.

(Peggy Billings, Consultation on Women Political Prisoners, May 1978)

The following is the full text of a statement adopted by the World Council of Churches in 1977:

...the emphasis of the Gospel is on the value of all human beings in the sight of God, on the atoning and redeeming work of Christ that has given to humanity true dignity, on love as the motive for action, and on love for one's neighbor as the practical expression of an active faith in Christ. We are members one of another, and when one suffers all are hurt.

(Consultation on Human Rights and Christian Responsibility, St. Polten, Austria, 1974)

The thirtieth meeting of the World Council of Churches' Central Committee (Geneva, 28 July—6 August 1977) has heard the words of its moderator, who, with deep sorrow, directed its attention to "a steady increase in reports of violation of human rights, and in the use of torture in an increasing number of countries of the world." Then the General Secretary called it

to "a style of thinking and of being which is a prerequisite for furthering the unity, witness and service of the people of God according to God's purpose." One essential element of this is a determination "to be true, and live the truth." "Being human," he said, "means to uncover things, to bring them to light, to disclose them, to deprive them of their hiddenness, to bring them into consciousness."

We are called to bear witness to the light which has come into the world through our Lord Jesus Christ. At the same time, we know "the judgement, that the light has come into the world, and men loved darkness more than light, because their deeds were evil. For everyone who does evil hates the light, lest his deeds be exposed." (John 3:19-20)

Today we stand under God's judgement, for in our generation the darkness, deceit and inhumanity of the torture chamber have become a more widespread and atrocious reality than at any other time in history. No human practice is so abominable, nor so widely condemned. Yet physical and mental torture and other forms of cruel and inhuman treatment are now being applied systematically in many countries, and practically no nation can claim to be free of them.

Next year the world will be called upon to mark the thirtieth anniversary of the adoption, on December 10, 1948, by the United Nations General Assembly, of the Universal Declaration of Human Rights. The preamble to that Declaration states that "recognition of the inherent dignity and of the equal and inalienable rights of all members of the human family is the foundation of freedom, justice and peace in the world."

The World Council of Churches Nairobi Assembly has urged us to hold high this concern for justice, to work for the implementation of the causes of violations of human rights.

The struggle to abolish torture involves "work at the most basic level towards a society without unjust structures" (Nairobi Assembly, Section V Report, par. 13). Torture is most likely to occur in societies which are characterized by injustice, but it can also happen in situations where most rights are protected. While torture is sometimes applied to common prisoners, the victims are most likely persons who have become involved in the struggle for justice and human rights in their own societies, people who have had the courage to voice the needs of the people. In the face of political opposition, rulers of an increasing number of countries have decreed emergency laws in which the basic guarantee of habeas corpus is suspended. Detainees are forbidden contact with a defense lawyer, their families, religious leaders, or others, creating conditions propitious for torture. Under the pretext of "national security," many states today subordinate human dignity to the selfish interests of those in power.

Given the tragic dimensions of torture in our world, we urge the churches to take this thirtieth anniversary year as a special occasion to lay bare the practice of, complicity in, and the propensity to torture which exist in our nations. Torture is epidemic, breeds in the dark, in silence. We call upon the churches to bring its existence into the open, to break the silence, to reveal the persons and structures of our societies which are responsible for this most dehumanizing of all violations of human rights.

We recognize that there remain, even among the churches, certain differences of interpretation of human rights, and that sometimes different priorities are set for the implementation of human rights according to varying socio-economic, political and cultural contexts. But on the point of torture there can be no difference of opinion. The churches together can and must become major forces for the abolition of torture.*

We therefore urge the churches to:

1. a) intensify their efforts to inform their members and the people of their nations about the provisions of the Universal Declaration of Human Rights, and especially of its Article 5 which reads:

No one shall be subjected to torture or to cruel, inhuman or degrading treatment or punishment.

b) continue and intensify their efforts to cause their governments to ratify the International Covenants on Economic, Social and Cultural Rights, and on Civil and Political Rights adopted by the United Nations General Assembly, December 16, 1966. Special efforts should be made to achieve the ratification of the "Optional Protocol" of the Covenant on Social and Political Rights *by which states agree to allow to be considered communications from individuals subject to their jurisdiction who claim to be victims of a violation of the rights set out in that Covenant by their own state.* Similarly, attention of governments should be called to the importance of ratifying specifically Article 41 of the Covenant on Civil and Political Rights, by which a state can express its willingness to allow other nations to raise questions through a careful procedure, about its compliance with the provisions of this Covenant, including its Article 7 which prohibits torture or cruel, inhuman or degrading treatment or punishment.

c) inform their members and the people of their nations of the contents of the "Declaration on the Protection of All Persons from Being Subjected to Torture and Other Cruel, Inhuman and Degrading Treatment or Punishment" unanimously adopted by the United Nations General Assembly on December 9, 1975.

---

* Note: The United Nations Declaration on the Protection of All Persons from Being Subjected to Torture and Other Cruel, Inhuman or Degrading Treatment or Punishment defines torture as:

1. Any act by which severe pain or suffering, whether physical or mental, is intentionally inflicted by or at the instigation of a public official on a person for such purposes as obtaining from him (her) or a third person information or confession, punishing him (her) for an act he (she) has committed or is suspected of having committed, or intimidating him (her) or other persons. It does not include pain or suffering arising only from, inherent in or incidental to, lawful sanctions to the extent consistent with the Standard Minimum Rules for the Treatment of Prisoners.

2. Torture constitutes an aggravated and deliberate form of cruel, inhuman or degrading treatment or punishment.

d) study and seek the application at all levels of governments of the "Standard Minimum Rules for the Treatment of Prisoners" adopted on August 30, 1955, by the First United Nations Congress on the Prevention of Crime and the Treatment of Offenders. [Ed. note: Approved by the Economic and Social Council in 1957 and again in 1977, Resolution 2076 (LXII).]

e) study and seek the application of "Declaration of Tokyo: Guidelines for Medical Doctors Concerning Torture and Other Cruel, Inhuman or Degrading Treatment or Punishment in Relation to Detention and Imprisonment" adopted by the twenty-ninth World Medical Assembly in Tokyo, October 1975.

2. Seek to ensure the compliance of their governments with the provisions of these important international instruments, recognizing that while the Declarations are not legally binding, they do represent a large international consensus and carry very substantial moral weight.

3. Express their solidarity with churches and people elsewhere in their struggle to have these provisions strictly applied in their own countries.

4. Urge their governments to contribute positively to the current effort of the United Nations to develop a body of principles for the protection of all persons under any form of detention or imprisonment, and to strengthen the existing procedures for the implementation of the "Standard Minimum Rules," and of the World Health Organization to develop a "Code of Medical Ethics Relevant to the Protection of Detained Persons Against Torture and Other Cruel, Inhuman or Degrading Treatment or Punishment."

5. Work for the elaboration by the United Nations of a Convention on the Protection of All Persons Against Torture.

6. Encourage other initiatives to establish an international strategy to fight against torture and to create an efficient international machinery to ban torture.

7. Ensure that law enforcement officials, members of the military and of special security branches, members of the medical profession and others be informed of the above-mentioned international standards and to press for their non-participation in torture, and their non-complicity with others directly involved.

8. Work against any further international commerce in torture techniques or equipment and against the development in the scientific community of even more sophisticated techniques of physical or mental torture.

9. Seek access to places of detention and interrogation centres in order to ensure that persons held there are not mistreated.

10. Be especially attentive to the fact that torture most often occurs after secret detention, abduction and subsequent disappearance of victims, and see to it that special rapid and appropriate measures be taken to locate them and to provide legal protection for such persons by the competent authorities.

Questions for Reflection

1. Explain the following sentence from the WCC Statement: "While torture is sometimes applied to common prisoners, the victims are most likely persons who have become involved in the struggle for justice and human rights in their own societies, people who have had the courage to voice the needs of the people." Why would people who struggle for human rights and justice be imprisoned and tortured?

2. Can you list specific cases which would illustrate the statement in question #1? Do the media to which you have access deal with this issue? How?

3. Consider the words at the beginning of the World Council of Churches' Statement: "We are members one of another, and when one suffers all are hurt." Do you agree with this quotation? If it is true, how do we stop the suffering?

Exercises for Reflection

1. Have you ever seen this statement before? Has your denomination done anything about it? Do you feel that your denomination should be involved? What steps would you take to involve your denomination or your local church? List them.

2. Get in touch with Amnesty International, a worldwide movement working on behalf of Prisoners of Conscience, men and women imprisoned because of their beliefs, color, ethnic origin, sex, language or religion, provided they have neither used nor advocated violence. Ask the organization what you can do to work with them. (Amnesty International, 2101 Algonquin Avenue, P. O. Box 6033, Ottawa, Ontario K2A ITI. National Office, 2112 Broadway, New York, New York 10023. Western Regional Office, 3618 Sacramento Street, San Francisco, California 94118.)

3. Get in touch with International Defense and Aid Fund for Southern Africa, a worldwide movement whose aims and objectives are stated as follows:

"In order to assist in the development of a non-racial society in Southern Africa based on a democratic way of life, the Fund exists to:

1. Aid, defend and rehabilitate the victims of unjust legislation and oppressive and arbitrary procedures.

2. Support their families and dependents.

3. Keep the conscience of the world alive to the issues at stake."

Ask them what you can do to work with them. (International Defense and Aid Fund for Southern Africa, P. O. Box 17, Cambridge, Massachusetts 02138.)

Preparing for Effective Witness: Further Reading

Chapter 1, pp. 18-21 and Chapter 2, pp. 47-50 in *Paradox and Promise in Human Rights* by Peggy Billings.

Resources

"The Politics of Torture"—This powerful documentary underscores the realities of President Carter's far-from-absolute human rights policy and the shortcomings of Congressional actions, using as examples the Philippines, Chile and Iran, all allies of the United States with long records of human rights abuses. 55 minutes. Available from California Newsreel, 630 Natoma St., San Francisco, CA 94103.

CHAPTER 4
ALIENS
MIA ADJALI

Article 13

An alien lawfully in the territory of **a State Party to the present Covenant may be** *expelled therefrom only* **in pursuance of a decision reached in** *accordance with law* **and shall, except where compelling reasons of national security otherwise require, be allowed to submit the reasons against his (her) expulsion and to have his (her) case reviewed by, and be represented for the purpose before, the competent authority or a person or persons especially designated by the competent authority.**

International Covenant on Civil and Political Rights (Italics added)

The human rights situation in the world today is dramatized by the millions of people who have to search for their freedom, work, and mere survival in other countries than their own. They have emigrated because of economic, social or political pressures. They have become aliens in other lands. While international discussions concerning human rights today sound promising for them, they are primarily dictated by the national self-interest of the host countries and fail, in practice, to measure up to their rhetoric.

Migrant workers, undocumented workers, and refugees are all aliens with different legal status. However, their situations have similar causes and effects. Their common characteristic is that they suffer their fate for no other reason than the fact that they belong to a deprived group in their societies of origin. The deprivation can have an economic, social or political overtone but the fact of belonging to a certain group is cause enough to produce the exodus which transforms them into aliens. Governmental policies and practices toward all three categories promise rights and democracy,* but deliver little. Racist attitudes and structures in both Canada and the United States have some

share in the blame. A greater proportion of aliens than in the past now come from Asia or Latin America and the Caribbean. In addition, the media have tended to cast a negative light on these aliens and contributed to a general societal mistrust and suspicion.

Migrant Workers

The United Nations has been worried about the present image of migrant workers. It has urged both the International Labor Organization (ILO) and the United Nations Educational, Scientific and Cultural Organization (UNESCO) to disseminate "information calculated to eliminate stereotypes and prejudices" which continue to lead to discrimination against migrant workers in the countries in which they work.

Unemployment in Third World countries has increased and their people have become migrant workers (with documents or without) in the highly industrialized countries. In the United States people in this category are hired for a specific type of work for a predetermined period of time. This seasonal labor is subject to regulations which permit a certain control over the conditions under which these workers work. In 1977 the United Nations General Assembly noted that the problem of migrant workers was of "major importance to many countries...becoming increasingly serious in certain regions and that the Commission on Human Rights and other relevant organs of the United Nations should take immediate measures to

---

Three persons have helped me to write this piece and I am grateful for their ideas and research: Arturo Chacon is Director of the Ecumenical Forum in Toronto, Canada; Susan Susman is a lawyer specializing in immigration law; Sharon Ham was an intern in Ms. Susman's office during the summer of 1978.

* In accordance with the Convention and Protocol relating to the Status of Refugees ratified by both Canada (which has incorporated the provisions in its Immigration Act of 1976) and the United States (the U.S. has only ratified the Protocol but the Protocol incorporates most of the Articles of the Convention), and in accordance

with the generally accepted resolutions on Migrant Workers of the United Nations.

ensure the human rights and dignity of all migrant workers."[1]

Undocumented Workers

Those workers who have no documents are better known in journalistic circles as illegal aliens. Some estimates put the rate of illegal aliens as double that of legal ones in the United States. In Canada the figure is much smaller, especially since the Immigration Act of 1976 established stricter controls on people entering the country. There is the usual complaint that the illegal aliens take away jobs from the rest of the population. This assertion seems to be unrealistic because the undocumented workers have jobs at the bottom of the scale, sometimes for half the minimum wage, and without other compensations like health insurance or social security. These conditions are not likely to be accepted by residents who know the rights which the undocumented worker dare not claim. Hence the complaint rings as a hollow one and only masks the fact that the recipient countries are in search of cheap labor or have jobs that the other members of the society are unwilling to do.

Undocumented workers are also accused of being a drain on the economy. And yet according to a 1976 study, funded by the United States Department of Labor, of the undocumented workers apprehended by the Immigration and Naturalization Service (INS), 77 percent paid social security tax and 73 percent paid federal income tax, while only .05 percent (five people out of 10,000) received welfare assistance, 1.3 percent received food stamps, and 3.9 percent collected one or more week(s) of unemployment compensation. In addition to being tax-paying members of the United States society, undocumented workers create jobs, since their consumer needs for housing, food, and services must be met.

Economic problems, far from being caused by undocumented workers, come from economic recessions, changes in technology and automation, and geographic relocation of major factories in search of unorganized (and therefore cheaper) labor and better tax breaks. To blame the undocumented workers for the economic ills of North America only draws attention away from the real causes of the problem.

The Cry for Justice

The case of migrant workers, lawfully admitted, differs little. They also are a convenient scapegoat for problems of unemployment in the United States or Canada. They too have little protection in the areas of

1. UN General Assembly Resolution 32/120, December 16, 1977.

health, social security, education for their children, and actual income. They too suffer exploitation to such an extent that their cause has become the cause of concerned people everywhere as already indicated by the 1977 UN General Assembly resolution.

In the United States legislation is pending for both documented and undocumented immigrants. However, the legislation fails to address the root causes of migration and sidesteps the responsibility of the government for the immigrants themselves, and the conditions which caused them to leave their homes. This is particularly evident in the numerical limitations imposed on immigration and in proposals for harsher restrictions on lawful entry into the United States. In 1965 for example, the quota of 120,000 for immigrants from the Western Hemisphere barred many Mexican workers seeking entry into the United States. The present quota of 170,000 for the Western Hemisphere (with a 20,000 maximum from any one country) ignores the fact that U.S. corporate interests and investments in many Third World countries have helped shape the economies of those countries, taking out large profits and raw materials to the detriment of the self-sufficiency of the local population. The unemployment created in those countries fosters increased migration.

The proposed legislation to stem the influx of immigrants makes it unlawful for an employer to hire an alien who is not a permanent resident or has not received INS permission to work. This system, called "employer sanctions," will encourage discrimination because employers will be reluctant to hire any Spanish-speaking or foreign-born citizen who does not carry proof of his/her citizenship at all times.

This is comparable to recently enacted Canadian legislation which prohibits foreign workers from staying in Canada without a work permit—and it marks a drastic change from Canada's virtual open-door policy prior to 1972.

In the United States a pending bill (Senate Bill S.2048) and its proposed amendment would impose a five-year residency requirement on permanent resident aliens as a condition for eligibility for social security insurance benefits, and would impose a binding five-year support agreement on the sponsors of immigrants. This means that any and every expense which an alien permanent resident may encounter—including emergency hospital bills—must be guaranteed in advance by the sponsoring relative or friend for a period of at least five years. This discriminates against poor and working class people trying to reunite their families. For them such a financial commitment might

18

be impossible.

President Carter's proposed "amnesty" for undocumented aliens who have been in the United States for substantial periods of time is currently under discussion in Congress. Because of the great fanfare with which it was announced by the media, it has already become a trap for many aliens who turned themselves in expecting "amnesty," only to find themselves under deportation proceedings.

Two kinds of amnesty are proposed in the bill. First, permanent resident visas will be granted to eligible aliens who arrived in the United States before January 1, 1970, and who have lived here continuously since their arrival. The burden is on the individual to come forth and prove the required residency and other aspects of eligibility. Second, "temporary resident status" until 1984 may be given to aliens who came to the United States between January 1, 1970 and January 1, 1977. Temporary residents, however, will not be permitted to bring their families here, and would not be eligible to receive any social benefits (such as Aid to Families with Dependent Children, Supplemental Security Income, or Food Stamps), although they would be required to pay taxes. The status of these temporary resident aliens after 1984 has not yet been decided.

The permanent resident status which would be granted to those with seven years of residence and other (as yet unspecified) qualifications, unfortunately rules out the majority of undocumented workers here. According to a 1976 Department of Labor study, of the people apprehended by the INS as undocumented aliens, few had been in the country longer than one or two years.

In the long and frustrating effort to achieve a meaningful amnesty proposal, community and immigration groups have historically advocated *unconditional* amnesty as the only possible program to fulfill the purpose in fact and not just in name. Many workers, lawyers, legal workers and other concerned people around the country have organized in opposition to the Carter proposal's creation of "temporary worker" status (similar to the German "guest worker" laws) and in favor of the rights of aliens to work and bring their families here.

Refugees

There has been much discussion recently in international forums on the rights of refugees. The policies and laws of the host (recipient) countries toward these people frequently reflect security and economic interests rather than humanitarian concerns. The case of refugees * is becoming a thorny issue in a world which is producing them at a faster rate than the institutional arrangements in existence can handle. Despite international agreements which theoretically provide broad protection for the civil and political rights of those seeking asylum, priority is still given to national security. Article 32 of the International Convention Relating to the Status of Refugees, mentioned earlier, addresses this concern by prohibiting the arbitrary expulsion of refugees who have already been lawfully admitted into the host country, "except where compelling reasons of national security otherwise require." This same caution is found in Article 13 of the Covenant on Civil and Political Rights (see preface of chapter) and applies to all aliens.

However inclusive the definition of national security in a society is, it is hoped that it would not have adverse effects on the human rights of the aliens in that society. Nevertheless, since the Second World War the national security doctrine has taken precedence over the need to secure the human rights of aliens. In the United States and Canada the implementation of the national security doctrine has been coined in terms of concern for "internal security." In turn, the concern for internal security finds its way into legislation related to immigration. For example, in Canada the Immigration Act of 1976 has provisions for "withholding of information which affects aliens for reasons of national security" or impeding the entrance to the territory of persons who, "there are reasonable grounds to believe, will engage in activities detrimental to it...."

There are some persons who become refugees because of economic oppression. Pending legislation in the United States Congress underlines the economic interests at stake. One such bill would bar asylum to persons if their primary motives were economic, even though they also had a legitimate fear of persecution. In countries whose economies and dictatorships are propped with United States aid, the question is a delicate one, and those fleeing are likely to be barred. This is true, for example, for the more than one thousand Haitian refugees who have come to the United States in small boats, fleeing persecution,

* The Convention and Protocol Relating to the Status of Refugees define a refugee as any person who "owing to well-founded fear of being persecuted for reasons of race, religion, nationality, membership in a particular social group or political opinion, is outside the country of his (her) nationality and is unable or, owing to such fear is unwilling to avail him (her)self of the protection of that country, or who not having a nationality and being outside the country of his (her) former habitual residence as a result of such events, is unable or owing to such fear, is unwilling to return to it." (Article 1, par. 2)

sometimes in the form of enforced unemployment in Haiti.

In any case, few of those who request political asylum actually receive it in the United States. In fiscal year 1976, 2,733 people applied for asylum; only 590 were granted it, and most of those were from Communist or Communist-dominated countries or the Middle East. Only a few of the refugees fleeing right-wing dictatorships and regimes in Latin America have been permitted to enter, and they have come in on emergency grants or exceptions to the law. Recently the Secretary of State requested "parole visas" (asylum or entry for the duration of an emergency situation) for 6,000 additional Soviet and Eastern European refugees for the last half of fiscal year 1978, while the Attorney General asked for parole, in March 1978, for only 55 political prisoners and refugees with their dependents from repressive regimes in Latin America. (A proposal to permit four or five hundred Latin American parolees and their families into the United States has been stalled for several months while the State and Justice Departments wrangle over regulations.)

Every human being has a right to a place in the world where he or she can live safely. First comes the right to live* where that person is. If that right is violated, then comes a right to live safely somewhere else. Only concerned citizens can move the "government machinery" to act more speedily and with greater justice.

Questions for Reflection

1. Are people in the United States and Canada being actively involved in the immigration debate? What do *you* know about it?

2. Is our nation without racial, political, national, or religious bias? What do our immigration policies indicate about us as a nation in this regard?

3. What are the reasons which force people to flee their country? What refugees have come to the United States or Canada in the last five years? Why were they refugees? How did the United States or Canada receive them? Were all persons who tried to take refuge in the U.S. or Canada given visas to enter? (See Chapter 14.)

4. How do you feel about undocumented workers? Should they be given amnesty? Discuss your feelings.

5. What do you know about migrant labor? What rights do you feel these people should have?

Exercises for Reflection

1. At the opening of the World Conference to Combat Racism and Racial Discrimination held in August 1978 in Geneva, UN Secretary General Kurt Waldheim urged participants at the conference "to consider ways and means to insure the cessation of all discriminatory measures against migrant workers and the promotion and protection of human rights of national, ethnic, and other minorities." Recognizing that governments can act against discrimination, the Secretary General pointed to "an equal need for action at the local or grass roots level." In this instance, he reminded us that "Non-Governmental Organizations can play a vital role by mobilizing public opinion and by initiating programs of information and education to advance the cause of social justice."

We must all understand, he said, that "many of the problems of minorities seeking better lives in other parts of the world have their source in the legacy of colonialism and in the intolerable condition under which hundreds of millions of people are forced to live in the new and developing country. The majority there is constantly on the verge of starvation and must cope with grievous inequities and lack of opportunity." The Secretary General emphasized "the overall need to accelerate Economic and Social Development as a means of promoting and protecting Human Rights."

What is your reaction to the words of Dr. Waldheim? Could some of his feelings toward migrant workers also apply to undocumented workers and refugees in the United States and Canada? In what way? What do you think should be the role of the church in answering Dr. Waldheim's plea to NGOs? What is your denomination or the Council of Churches doing about these issues? What would you do about these issues?

Preparing for Effective Witness: Further Reading
"Freedom of Movement," Chapter 14.

Resources
NACLA Report on the Americas—November-December 1977, Vol. XI, No. 8. Special issue on "Caribbean Migration: Contract Labor in U.S. Agriculture." Available from North American Congress on Latin America, Box 57, Cathedral Station, New York, N.Y.

"A Day Without Sunshine"—A documentary on the plight of migrant workers in the citrus groves of Florida, this film counterpoints closeups of working families—their strenuous labors, their financial precariousness, their powerlessness—with comments from the industry and the government which supports that industry. 60 minutes. Available from CC Films, Rm. 860, 475 Riverside Drive, New York, N.Y. 10027. Sale $450; rental $45.

CHAPTER 5
TO VOTE AND PARTICIPATE IN PUBLIC AFFAIRS
ROXANNE COOP

Article 25
Every citizen shall have the right and the opportunity, without any of the distinctions mentioned in article 2, and without unreasonable restrictions:

(a) *To take part in the conduct of public affairs,* **directly or through freely chosen representatives,**

(b) *To vote and to be elected* **at genuine periodic elections which shall be by universal and equal suffrage and shall be held by secret ballot, guaranteeing the free expression of the will of the electors;**

(c) *To have access, on general terms of equality, to public service* **in his (her) country.**

International Covenant on
Civil and Political Rights (Italics added)

Micronesia is the last remaining trust territory in the world, one of the eleven formed by the United Nations after World War II to guarantee the right of self-determination for peoples who had been innocently caught up in the power struggles of imperial nations.*

"Micronesia" refers to the "tiny islands" of the western Pacific Ocean just north of the equator. The name is used interchangeably with "United States Trust Territory" to designate three major island chains—the Carolines, the Marshalls and the Marianas—which dot an ocean area the size of the continental United States. Technically Micronesia also includes Guam, a U.S. colony in the Marianas group; the Gilbert Islands, a self-governing territory of the United Kingdom; and Nauru, an independent nation.

A trust territory is theoretically different from a colony in that sovereignty resides with the indigenous people rather than with the administering authority. Micronesians have endured both conditions during a 400-year history of domination by foreign powers. Spain "owned" the island from 1520 to 1898, forfeiting Guam to the United States during the Spanish-American War. At that time Germany "bought" Micronesia from Spain, losing it in turn to Japan at the beginning of World War I. Following the First World War, Japan administered the islands under a League of Nations mandate, which attributed sovereignty to the Micronesians. The United States continued to govern Guam as an "unincorporated territory."

The bloody sacrifice of American soldiers during World War II gave many Americans the sense that they had somehow purchased the island with their lives. However, the agreement under the United Nations Trusteeship System continued to protect the sovereignty of the Micronesian people.[1] The United States became accountable to the United Nations for the future of Micronesians and was obliged to promote their progressive development toward self-government or independence.

More than 30 years later, in the spring of 1978, the

Roxanne Coop worked in the South Pacific Islands for six years in leadership development for the Program Agency of the United Presbyterian Church, USA. When writing this paper, Roxanne was working with DOM-NCCC office for East Asia and the Pacific.

*One of the basic objectives of the United Nations Trusteeship System is: "To promote the political, economic, social and educational advancement of the inhabitants of the trust territories, and their progressive development towards self-government or independence as may be appropriate to the particular circumstances of each territory and its peoples and the freely expressed wishes of the peoples concerned, and as may be provided by the terms of each trusteeship agreement." (Article 76, Chapter XII, UN Charter)

1. Territories held under League of Nations mandate were transferred to the United Nations Trusteeship System (Article 77, Ch. XII, UN Charter).

Congress of Micronesia—the duly elected legislature of the Trust Territory—accused the United States government of interfering in the process of self-determination. A protest to the United Nations Security Council seriously embarrassed the United States and underscored the fact that the U.S. defense interests were impinging on the sovereignty of the Micronesian people.

The act of self-determination in question was a territory-wide referendum on the proposed Constitution of the Federated States of Micronesia. Its passage would confirm the sovereignty and independence of the ratifying districts. No one doubted that every Micronesian would be entitled to vote, or that they would be free to participate in public debate. But many feared that United States strategic interests would upset the process of political education leading to the referendum.

Micronesian indignation over public statements by United States officials commenting on the proposed constitution led them to seek close supervision of the referendum by the Security Council as "the only way to ensure that the proper conditions exist for all the people of the Trust Territory to exercise their right to vote freely in the referendum."

In a petition to the Security Council, the Congress of Micronesia claimed that "anything less than active supervision by the United Nations during the referendum and observation during the period of political education prior to it will invite further intimidation of Micronesian voters both from within and without the Territory."

What brought the United States to such an awkward pass, where it appeared to be threatening the right to vote of 115,000 people living in scattered islands of the Central Pacific? A clue might be found by looking back a few years to 1975, when the United States Congress ratified a covenant establishing the Commonwealth of the Northern Marianas, permanently annexing territory for the first time since the acquisition of the Virgin Islands in 1917. The question about United States intentions with regard to the whole of Micronesia had crystallized. The United States would fragment the territory and annex a part of it to guarantee U.S. security needs. While the agreement with the Marianas alleviated United States anxiety about future military-base locations in the Pacific, defense strategy still demanded secure positions in the Marshalls, where the Kwajelein Missile-Testing Range is located, and Palau, in the Western Carolines.

The United States Trust Territory is unique not only in being the last remaining one, but also in being the only one designated a strategic trust territory.[2] The United States, faced with the dilemma of wanting to appear non-colonial yet wanting to attach the islands for national security purposes, concluded a special agreement with the Security Council in 1947. The agreement, which recognized the islands as having strategic value for U.S. security and world peace, granted the United States almost complete control over the territory, short of actual integration.

Since the establishment of military installations was permissible, the United States proceeded to use the territory for nuclear weapons tests, naval and air bases, missile testing and germ warfare experimentation. Atmospheric tests on Bikini atoll in the 1950s vaporized one island. An errant radioactive cloud severely damaged the people of two other islands in the Marshalls group. Radioactive contamination of Bikini island has resulted in the accumulation of abnormal amounts of plutonium, strontium and cesium in the bodies of residents. They were returned to their island with assurances of safety in 1969 and forced to leave again in 1978. Radiation entered the bodies of the people of Bikini through the food chain.

The United States made heavy investments in public services, such as health and education, neglecting the development of an island-based economy. In the manner of a colonial power, the United States imposed its own educational system, wrapping Micronesians in a cocoon of values belonging to the dominant culture. Students moved through an academic stream, expecting high-salaried jobs in government offices. Micronesians became trapped by a system that exiled them from the subsistence economy and the cultural values that once sustained them. At the same time, they acquired an appetite for American manufactured goods which they could not afford. Imports increased drastically to support the consumer economy generated by the presence of thousands of United States military and civilian personnel.

The obligation of the trustee was to guide Micronesians toward self-government or independence. But this clashed with United States policy which fostered dependence and gradually reduced the possibility of a real choice.

In 1969, when the United States and the Congress of Micronesia began talks to negotiate a future politi-

_____
2. "There may be designated, in any trusteeship agreement, a strategic area or areas which may include part or all of the trust territory..." (Article 82, Ch. XII of UN Charter).

cal status for the Trust Territory, it was clear that the U.S. government opposed independence. Micronesians, by this time highly conscious politically, declared their non-negotiable assumptions: they were sovereign, possessing the right of self-determination, the right to choose independence or self-government in association with any nation, and the right to adopt their own constitution.

Negotiators focused on "free association" as the status option most likely to accommodate both United States strategic requirements and the island need for financial support. In accordance with the United Nations concept of free association, certain rights and responsibilities would be given to the United States government by the people of Micronesia through an exercise of their sovereign right of self-determination.

A Draft Compact of Free Association was eventually initiated at Saipan in 1976 after seven years of frequent standoffs between the representatives of two sovereign peoples. The Draft Compact gave the future government of Micronesia "full responsibility for, and authority over, the internal affairs of Micronesia" and gave the United States government control over defense and foreign affairs.

One condition would continue to plague negotiators, however. The compact could be terminated by mutual consent at any time but could not be terminated unilaterally until after the first 15 years. This section contradicted a longstanding negotiating principle of the Micronesians: that the right of unilateral termination at any time was essential to the preservation of Micronesia's sovereignty. The Draft Compact of Free Association provided for nothing more than an interim status, allowing for the possibility of independence at a later date.

Although most Micronesians acknowledged that their destiny was in association with the United States, their sentiment for independence flamed again and again and burned steadily in the Constitutional Convention in 1975. Article II, as drafted, defined the "Supremacy" of the proposed constitution as follows: "This Constitution is the expression of the sovereignty of the people and is the supreme law of the Federated States of Micronesia. An act of the Government in conflict with this Constitution is invalid to the extent of the conflict."

As the political education process got underway and the referendum approached, the United States questioned the document, calling it incompatible with the Draft Compact for Free Association and urging the Congress of Micronesia to amend the proposed consti-

tution. When Micronesians refused to do so, the United States government intervened, first by suspending the Trust Territory's Education for Self-Government Program in order to reorganize it (a prerogative of the administering authority) and then by making public statements discouraging adoption of the proposed constitution. The United States believed that most Micronesians did not want independence anyway and that political education was not taking full account of the alternative status of free association, which had already been negotiated. Claiming interference, the Congress of Micronesia called a halt, suspended further status talks until after the referendum, and resolved to request the United Nations Security Council to monitor the political education process.

Toward a New Policy

When the President of the Senate and the Speaker of the House of Representatives of the Congress of Micronesia visited New York in order to petition the United Nations Security Council, the U.S. Office for Micronesia Status Negotiations announced a shift in its negotiating position. The United States had decided that it could separate the issue of defense interests from the issue of future political status for Micronesia. It offered to negotiate a new agreement of free association on a government-to-government basis after the referendum.

In a new statement of principles the United States requested authority over security and defense matters, asking that this authority be assured for 15 years. It granted Micronesians authority for foreign affairs, including marine resources. Perhaps most significant: the United States proposed an agreement which would permit unilateral termination of the free association political status at any time, subject to continuation of U.S. defense authority.

Micronesians—at this time represented by three future political status commissions (Congress of Micronesia and the separatist districts of Palau and the Marshalls)—accepted the new principles, clearing the way for the referendum.

In the constitutional referendum held on July 12, 1978, four districts of the Trust Territory ratified the Constitution of the Federated States of Micronesia, automatically creating a new government effective one year after the ratification. The separatist districts of the Marshalls and Palau rejected the constitution, establishing their independence from the Federated States. These two districts are now preparing their own constitutions, as well as continuing separate political status negotiations with the United States.

Questions for Reflection

1. Micronesians saw the right to vote as more than the right to cast a ballot. In the referendum to form their own government, they saw the right to vote as an expression of their own sovereignty. What is your understanding of sovereignty? Where does sovereignty reside? In individuals? In peoples? In nations? What does "national sovereignty" mean?

2. In the United States, Native Americans are citizens and have the right to vote. Yet they are struggling for sovereignty—for self-determination. What is the difference between the struggle of Native Americans and that of Micronesians? (See Chapter 1.)

3. Early in the future-political-status negotiations, the United States tried unsuccessfully to assume the right of eminent domain in order to guarantee land for military use. Henry Kissinger is popularly quoted as saying at the time, "There are only 90,000 people out there. Who gives a damn?" The U.S. had already used territory for nuclear weapons tests, naval and air bases, missile testing and germ warfare experimentation. Should the rights of any people (such as the Micronesians) be jeopardized for the sake of the "security" of another people (such as the people of the U.S.)? Discuss the UN Trusteeship System allowing for "strategic area or areas." Does this conflict with the right to self-determination of peoples?

Exercises for Reflection

1. Micronesians struggled for the right to vote but perhaps that was only symbolic of the right to self-determination. Discuss the full implications of the struggles in Micronesia. What will the Micronesians have achieved once independent? It is often said that political independence is only the first step in the liberation and development of a society. What is meant by such a statement?

In October of 1978 the National Council of Churches of Christ in the USA (Committee for East Asia and the Pacific) called for a one-day meeting to focus on Micronesia. You will better understand the obstacles facing the Micronesians by carefully considering a preliminary listing of problems in the memo announcing the meeting:

> The United States' 30-year period of trusteeship in the Pacific Islands is drawing to a close.... The pressure is on for a conclusion of the trusteeship agreement by 1981. The constitutional referendum held July 12 resulted in the separation of Palau and the Marshall Islands districts from the rest of the trust territory....Future political status negotiations resume first place on the diplomats' agenda, now tripled in scope for the U.S. Radiation poisoning in the Marshalls continues to plague the health and social welfare of present and future generations. Law of the Sea Conference negotiations, so vital to Micronesian economy, await resolution.... Federal food, job and welfare programs extend themselves tenuously into the lives of Micronesian people.... Defense and security remain paramount interests behind U.S. policy.

2. In 1945 the United Nations Charter made important provisions for certain colonized territories through its Trusteeship System. However, many other countries such as Zimbabwe (Southern Rhodesia) did not fall under this system. What mechanism did the United Nations set up to help other non-self-governing territories? Do some research on developments in the United Nations since its founding. The membership of the organization has tripled in size since 1945. List three of the nations which are new members and research how they became independent.

Preparing for Effective Witness: Further Reading
"Self-Determination," Chapter 1.

Resources
Micronesia:Trust Betrayed by Donald F. McHenry. Available from Carnegie Endowment for International Peace, 11 Dupont Circle, N.W., Washington, D.C. 20036. Cost: $4.95.

Basic Facts About the United Nations, E.77.1.3, United Nations New York. Available from Sales Section, Room A-3315, United Nations, New York, New York 10017. Cost: $1.50.

Bulletins, Micronesia Support Committee, 1212 University Avenue, Honolulu, Hawaii 96826. Contributions requested.

Office for East Asia and the Pacific, Division of Overseas Ministries, National Council of Churches, 475 Riverside Drive, New York, New York 10027.

For further information on the United Nations, write the United Nations Office of Public Information, United Nations, New York, New York 10017 or UNA-USA, 300 East 42nd Street, New York, New York 10017 or UNA Central Office in Canada, 63 Sparks Street, Ottawa, Ontario KIP 5A6, Canada.

CHAPTER 6
A CHARTER FOR RACIAL JUSTICE POLICIES IN AN INTERDEPENDENT GLOBAL COMMUNITY
WOMEN'S DIVISION, BOARD OF GLOBAL MINISTRIES
THE UNITED METHODIST CHURCH
APRIL 1978

Article 26

All persons are *equal before the law* and are entitled without any discrimination to the *equal protection of the law.* In this respect, the law shall prohibit any discrimination and guarantee to all persons equal and effective protection against discrimination on any ground such as race, colour, sex, language, religion, political or other opinion, national or social origin, property, birth or other status.

Article 27

In those States in which *ethnic, religious or linguistic minorities exist,* persons belonging to such minorities shall not be denied the right, in community with the other members of their group, *to enjoy their own culture, to profess and practise their own religion, or to use their own language.*

International Covenant on Civil and Political Rights (Italics added)

Women's Division, Board of Global Ministries
The United Methodist Church
April 1978

Because We Believe

1. that God is the Creator of all people and all are God's children in one family;
2. that racism is a rejection of the teachings of Jesus Christ;
3. that racism denies the redemption and reconciliation of Jesus Christ;
4. that racism robs all human beings of their wholeness and is used as a justification for social, economic and political exploitation;
5. that we must declare before God and before each other that we have sinned against our sisters and brothers of other races in thought, in word and in deed;
6. that in our common humanity in creation all women and men are made in God's image and all persons are equally valuable in the sight of God;
7. that our strength lies in our racial and cultural diversity and that we must work toward a world in which each person's value is respected and nurtured;
8. that our struggle for justice must be based on new attitudes, new understandings and new relationships and must be reflected in the laws, policies, structures and practices of both church and state;

WE COMMIT OURSELVES AS INDIVIDUALS AND AS A COMMUNITY TO FOLLOW JESUS

CHRIST IN WORD AND IN DEED AND TO STRUGGLE FOR THE RIGHTS AND THE SELF-DETERMINATION OF EVERY PERSON AND GROUP OF PERSONS. THEREFORE, AS UNITED METHODIST WOMEN IN EVERY PLACE ACROSS THE LAND...

We will UNITE OUR EFFORTS with all groups in the United Methodist Church

1. to eliminate all forms of institutional racism in the total ministry of the church with special attention given to those institutions which we support, beginning with their employment policies, purchasing practices and availability of services and facilities.

2. to create opportunities in local churches to deal honestly with the existing racist attitudes and social distance between members, deepening the Christian commitment to be the church where all racial groups and economic classes come together.

3. to increase our efforts to recruit women of all races into the membership of United Methodist Women and provide leadership development opportunities without discrimination.

4. to create workshops and seminars in local churches to study, understand and appreciate the historical and cultural contributions of each race to the church and community.

5. to increase local churches' awareness of the continuing needs for equal education, housing, employment and medical care for all members of the community and create opportunities to work for these things across racial lines.

6. to work for the development and implementation of national and international policies to protect the civil, political, economic, social and cultural rights of all people such as through support for the ratification of United Nations covenants on human rights.

7. to support and participate in the worldwide struggle for liberation in the church and community.

8. to support nomination and election processes which include all racial groups, employing a quota system until the time that our voluntary performance makes such practice unnecessary.

(The Women's Division of the Board of Global Ministries of The United Methodist Church calls with urgency on all units of United Methodist Women to study the principles and goals stated in this charter, looking toward early ratification by each jurisdiction and conference by March 1, 1980. Such ratification will constitute a commitment to work for the speedy implementation of these principles and goals within jurisdiction, conference, district and local units.)

History

Racism is the belief that one race is innately superior to all other races. In the United States, this belief has justified the conquest, enslavement and evangelizing of non-Europeans. During the early history of this country, Europeans assumed their civilization and religion were innately superior to those of both the original inhabitants of the United States and the Africans who were forcefully brought to these shores to be slaves. The myth of European superiority persisted and persists. Other people who came and who are still coming to the United States by choice or force encountered and encounter racism. Some of these people are the Chinese who built the railroads as indentured workers; the Mexicans whose lands were annexed; the Puerto Ricans, the Cubans, the Hawaiians and the Eskimos who were colonized; and the Filipinos, the Jamaicans and the Haitians who live on starvation wages as farm workers.

In principle, the United States has outlawed racial discrimination but, in practice, little has changed. Social, economic and political institutions still discriminate, although some institutions have amended their behavior by eliminating obvious discriminatory practices and choosing their language carefully. The institutional church, despite sporadic attempts to the contrary, also still discriminates.

The damage of years of exploitation has not been erased. A system designed to meet the needs of one segment of the population cannot be the means to the development of a just society for all. The racist system in the United States today perpetuates the power and control of those of European ancestry. It is often called "white racism." The fruits of racism are prejudice, bigotry, discrimination, and dehumanization. Consistently, Blacks, Hispanics, Asians, Native Americans and Pacific Islanders have been humiliated by being given inferior jobs, housing, education, medical services, transportation and public accommodation. With hopes deferred and rights still denied, the deprived and oppressed fall prey to a colonial mentality which acquiesces to the inequities, occasionally with religious rationalizations.

Racist presuppositions have been implicit in U.S. attitudes and policies toward Asia, Africa, the Middle East and Latin America. While proclaiming democracy, freedom and independence, the U.S. has been an ally and an accomplice to perpetuating inequality of the races and colonialism throughout the world. The history of The United Methodist Church and the history of the United States are intertwined. The "mission enterprise" of the churches in the United States and "westernization" went hand in hand, sustained in their belief of their superiority.

The history of United Methodist Women reflects its awareness of racism in both the church and society. United Methodist Women has struggled against racism for many years. In 1941, the Woman's Division of Christian Service of The Methodist Church adopted a policy of "holding its meetings only in places where all members of its group can be entertained without any form of racial discrimination." The Women's Council of the Evangelical United Brethren Church voted in 1955: "We know that Christian women can, by their attitudes and acts, exert a tremendous influence toward the lessening of racial tensions. Therefore, we urge all members of the Women's Society of World Service to work for right relationships in all areas of life through their local churches and in their community living. We urge the citizens of the United States of America to do all in their power to aid in the desegregation of public schools as decreed by the Supreme Court."

The Woman's Division of Christian Service continued its commitment to eliminate institutional racism. A Charter for Racial Policies was adopted in 1952. The present Charter of Racial Policies was adopted in 1962. At its annual meeting in 1973, the Women's Division adopted a strong objective to eliminate institutional racism in the total ministry of the Women's Division. In 1977, this objective was reaffirmed.

We are conscious that "we have sinned as our ancestors did; we have been wicked and evil" (Psalm 106:6, Today's English Version). We are called for a renewed commitment to the elimination of institutional racism. We affirm the 1976 General Conference Statement on The United Methodist Church and Race, which states unequivocally: "By biblical and theological precept, by the law of the Church, by General Conference pronouncement, and by episcopal expression, the matter is clear. With respect to race, the aim of The United Methodist Church is nothing less than an inclusive church in an inclusive society. The United Methodist Church, therefore, calls upon all its people to perform those faithful deeds of love and justice in both the church and community that will bring this aim into reality."

Exercises for Reflection

1. Define racism.

2. Define institutional racism.

3. Describe other discriminatory practices and beliefs such as sexism.

4. Reread Article 26 of the International Covenant on Civil and Political Rights at the beginning of this chapter. Can the socio-economic-political-cultural institutions and structures of the United States or Canada "guarantee to all persons equal and effective protection against discrimination on any ground such as race, colour, sex, language, religion, political or other opinion, national or social origin, property, birth or other status"? Discuss by critiquing an institution

you know well. People in the United States may wish to discuss the Supreme Court ruling on Allan P. Bakke vs. the University of California Medical School, June 28, 1978. The Supreme Court voted (5-4) to affirm a lower court order requiring the University of California Medical School to admit Allan Bakke. His suit had alleged "reverse discrimination" by the Medical School, since it had set a goal of 16 places (out of 100 each year) for admission of minorities from disadvantaged backgrounds through a special program. Separate consideration was thereby maintained for minority students, especially those victimized by racism. What have been the subsequent interpretations of the Supreme Court's ruling that race may, in fact, be taken into account in such situations? How are seemingly contradictory opinions being resolved in practice?

5. Reread Article 27 of the International Covenant on Civil and Political Rights at the beginning of this chapter. What are the implications for countries like the United States and Canada? How does the State assure that minorities "enjoy their own culture, profess and practise their own religion, or...use their own language"? Are the rights of individual members of minorities violated? If so, what is the best course of action to protect such individuals? Relate these questions to the introduction of Section I.

6. Do you feel that the Women's Division of the United Methodist Church was justified in adopting a Charter for Racial Justice Policies in an Interdependent Global Community? Make a list of your reasons.

How would you implement such policies in your church? In your community?

What are the international dimensions of such policies?

If you were to write a Statement on Racial Justice Policies, what would you include?

7. The United Nations held a World Conference to Combat Racism and Racial Discrimination, August 14-25, 1978, in Geneva, Switzerland. The Secretary-General Kurt Waldheim said in his opening statement:

> While apartheid* represents racial discrimination in a particularly stark form, it is unfortunately true that discrimination based on race, and especially on colour, prevails in other parts of the world. Wherever it exists, it entails the same personal suffering, the same emotional stress and the same injustice, and denies people equal opportunity for self-development and fulfillment. Such discrimination is totally contrary to the objectives for which the United Nations stands. It is also a source of danger to international stability and peace, both on the humanitarian and political levels, for racial discrimination, wherever it exists, is an affront to us all and a danger to the creation of a more equitable and peaceful world.

How do you feel about these words? Did your media cover this important conference? How did your gov-

* See Chapter 2.

28

ernment participate in the Conference? What decisions were taken at the Conference and how does your government intend to deal with the resolutions? Get in touch with your representatives in your national legislative body in Ottawa or Washington and ask them about this conference and their reaction to it.

8. Canada has ratified the International Convention on the Elimination of All Forms of Racial Discrimination. The United States has signed the Convention and submitted it to the U.S. Senate for ratification. What is the content of the Convention and what are its implications? (You should be able to obtain a copy of the Convention from government offices.) United States citizens might prefer to ask their senators for a copy of the Convention. At the same time, request their opinion on the Convention.

Preparing for Effective Witness: Further Reading

"United States and Canadian Domestic Policy and Human Rights," Chapter 4, pp.70-95 in *Paradox and Promise in Human Rights* by Peggy Billings.

"The Exploitation of the Covenant: The Abuses of Chosenness," Chapter 10, pp.67-74; "The Critique of the Covenant: The Social Contract Broken and Renewed," Chapter 11, pp. 75-83, in *The Liberating Bond...*by Wolfgang Roth and Rosemary Radford Ruether.

Resources

Human Rights in Canada: A Focus on Racism by Daniel G. Hill, 1977. Published by Social and Community Programs Department, Canadian Labour Congress, 15 Gervais Drive, Toronto, Ontario M3C 1Y8.

Council on Interracial Books for Children, 1841 Broadway, New York, New York 10023 has *Fact Sheets on Institutional Racism* ($1.00) and filmstrips, "From Racism to Pluralism" (sale cost $32.50) and "Understanding Institutional Racism" (sale cost $32.50). The two filmstrips would be $50.00 if purchased together.

REFLECTIONS ON SECTION I

HUMAN RIGHTS PERTAIN TO INDIVIDUALS
AND TO THE
HUMAN COLLECTIVES OF WHICH THEY ARE
A PART

Learning to Interpret the Signs of the Times

The United Nations is clear in the Preamble of the two Human Rights Covenants that "all members of the human family have inherent dignity and equal and inalienable rights" and that "these rights are derived from the inherent dignity of the human person." Further, the United Nations considers that its member States are obligated "to promote universal respect for, and observance of, human rights and freedoms...."

The implication is that nations are responsible for developing such structures and institutions as will assure the rights of everyone in the society. We must be responsible to hold our governments accountable to their commitments in human rights. In addition, Christians are accountable to God for their relationships to each other and to others. There are no greater commandments than "Love the Lord your God with all your heart, with all your soul, with all your mind, and with all your strength," and "Love your neighbour as yourself." (Mark 12:30-31)

Section I has not told the whole story. It has only hinted at some of the situations people face. Humanity continues to battle unjust and cruel relationships caused by colonialism, dehumanizing labor conditions, torture, economic deprivation and political repression leading to exile, the lack of freedom to participate in the political life of one's country, racism and apartheid. In each case described, there will be arguments on the analysis. Yet what cannot be denied is that people are hurting and are, in a variety of ways, claiming and struggling for the rights which the international community has agreed upon. To further understand the nature of the human rights struggles is to pursue and deepen the sketchy analysis given so far.

Where are people striving for self-determination? What are the obstacles? Where are people tortured and why? What other dehumanizing work situations do we know of? Political and economic refugees have fled to many parts of the world. What conditions exist in their countries leading to such exile? What conditions exist in the countries of their exile? How important is it to be able to vote and participate in public affairs? How can we eliminate racism and apartheid?

Christians should seek information from different sources and perspectives, mindful that those who dominate our societies have great influence on the data which daily comes to us through our newspapers, radios, and television, as well as public platforms and masses of literature. The Christian's bias is towards those who know their need of God; for the sorrowful; for those of a gentle spirit; for those who hunger and thirst to see right prevail; for those who show mercy; for those whose hearts are pure; for the peacemakers; and for those who have suffered persecution for the cause of right. (Matthew 5:3-10) To know "their data" Christians must be with them at all times living the hope and life for which Jesus died. A continuous task for Christians is to be alert to the "Signs of the Times" which will help us to interpret the present time and point to those who struggle to defend and promote human rights and freedoms.

"What hypocrites you are! You know how to interpret the appearance of earth and sky; how is it you cannot interpret this fateful hour?" (Luke 12:56) What did Jesus mean by this statement? Was he reminding us that we must at all times know our present reality and continually seek to be the human presence of God in this world? How do we know how to act as God would wish us to?

Throughout biblical history the people of God were reminded of the reality in which they lived and their disregard of the covenant they had with God. At those moments of crisis, prophets cried out the injustices perpetuated by the people. A good definition of a prophet has been given by Bernhard W. Anderson in *The Unfolding Drama of the Bible.* "The true prophet was one who interpreted the meaning of the historical crisis in the light of Israel's covenant loyalty. The prophets were not extremists who introduced radically new conceptions which broke with the past, nor were they reactionaries who merely repeated the old traditions in a new time. Rather, they spoke to the urgent and imperative present of the community by reinterpreting the meaning of the covenant traditions in the present crisis and by warning the people of the consequences of their action for the future."[1]

Your study group should be divided into two groups for an exercise to discern signs of the times. One group should turn to the Bible for an account of one "historical crisis." (You may decide to examine a favorite Old Testament story for this.) Prepare a presentation for the other half of the group, including the following elements:

1. Description of the reality of the time.

2. Description of positive signs of the times. Signs which indicate forces fostering just and loving relationships. Signs which indicate the promotion and defense of human rights.

3. Description of negative signs of the times. Signs which indicate forces of dehumanization. Signs which indicate violations of human rights.

4. Description of the elements in the people's "covenant loyalty" to God. What was the meaning of the covenant in that time? What did God demand? What was God's promise? What did the people do?

The second group should deal with reality today—a "present crisis"—and include the same elements as noted above. However, the questions are slightly different: What is the meaning of the covenant today? What does God demand? What is God's promise? What shall we do?

In the introduction to Section I, Dwain Epps notes that "we understand the gospel to call individuals into the whole—there to be instruments of humanization, liberation and change. The serious question facing the churches is how to manifest their concern for individuals who are integral parts of a large society. Clearly, no simplistic approach such as the individualistic one will permit effective action in societies that are increasingly complex."

How do our churches manifest their concern for individuals and for society?

How should our churches manifest their concern for individuals and for society?

1. Bernhard W. Anderson, *The Unfolding Drama of the Bible* (New York: Association Press, Third Printing, 1976), p. 50.

SECTION II

THE STRUGGLE FOR THE DEFENSE AND PROMOTION OF HUMAN RIGHTS INVOLVES RECOURSE TO POLITICAL ACTION

INTRODUCTION

The fact is that human relations are largely governed by the distribution of power in society. Therefore the rights of those who wield economic, cultural, political, or military power are rarely violated. It is those from whom power has been taken or withheld who suffer. Can human rights be realized without doing something to right the imbalance of power? Attempts are made. For example, to a member of the oppressed racial minority a measure of equality in employment or education is granted. But it cannot be assumed that by multiplying the amelioration of individual symptoms a basic social ill is cured. The racially, economically, and politically oppressed of the world are becoming aware of the insufficiency of palliatives. They see the need for changes in the structures of society in the direction of greater justice and equality. It is the task of the church, in defense of human rights, to lend support to these political efforts without which real guarantees for human rights are but illusions.

Dwain Epps

CHAPTER 7
TO RESTORE THE ECONOMIC HEALTH
OF THE COMMUNITY

Article 6

1. The States Parties to the present Covenant recognize the *right to work,* which includes the right of everyone to the opportunity to gain his (her) living by work which he (she) freely chooses or accepts, and will take appropriate steps to safeguard this right.

2. The steps to be taken by a State Party to the present Covenant to achieve the full realization of this right shall include technical and vocational guidance and training programmes, policies and techniques to achieve steady economic, social and cultural development and full and productive employment under conditions safeguarding fundamental political and economic freedoms to the individual.

Article 7

The States Parties to the present Covenant recognize the right of everyone to the *enjoyment of just and favourable conditions of work* which ensure, in particular:

(a) Remuneration which provides all workers, as a minimum, with:

(i) Fair wages and equal remuneration for work of equal value without distinction of any kind, in particular women being guaranteed conditions of work not inferior to those enjoyed by men, with equal pay for equal work;

(ii) A decent living for themselves and their families in accordance with the provisions of the present Covenant;

(b) Safe and healthy working conditions;

(c) Equal opportunity for everyone to be promoted in his (her) employment to an appropriate higher level, subject to no considerations other than those of seniority and competence;

(d) Rest, leisure and reasonable limitation of working hours and periodic holidays with pay, as well as remuneration for public holidays.

International Covenant on Economic,
Social and Cultural Rights (Italics added)

The following statement was developed by the Ecumenical Coalition of the Mahoning Valley in Youngstown, Ohio on November 29, 1977.

Our community was wounded on September 19. On that date, the Lykes Corporation announced its decision to close most of its Youngstown Sheet and Tube operations at its Campbell facility and several departments at Brier Hill and relocate its offices. This decision is costing our Valley a great deal in human suffering, economic health and lost confidence and

vitality. Five thousand of our neighbors will be out of work. An additional 10,000 jobs may be lost in the ripple effects of this decision. In addition, several local communities may be forced to cut back on essential services at a time when they are most needed. This blow to our community has generated shock, anger, and genuine fear.

We in the religious community are profoundly disturbed and troubled by this decision and its tragic consequences. We, therefore, wish to share with you our reflections on what these events mean for us and our community.

We are not experts in steel production or economic matters. We do not come with simple or easy answers. Rather, we come as pastors deeply concerned about the pain and fear now present in our community. We need to examine the causes of this crisis and how we might act to alleviate suffering. We also need to consider how we might be able to restore economic health in our Valley and how we can strive to insure that this distress will not happen again.

We believe that this action by the Lykes Corporation has meaning far beyond its own troubled financial affairs and even beyond the fate of its 5,000 local employees. This decision raises profound issues of corporate responsibility and justice. It poses an enormous challenge to the Youngstown community and to the nation.

We say this because the decision is the result of a way of doing business in this country that too often fails to take into account the human dimensions of economic action. Other companies are faced with similar decisions in this community and other cities across the nation. As religious leaders, we cannot ignore the moral and religious aspects of this crisis.

Some maintain that this decision is a private, purely economic judgment which is the exclusive prerogative of the Lykes Corporation. We disagree. This decision is a matter of public concern since it profoundly affects the lives of so many people as well as the future of Youngstown and the Mahoning Valley.

The costs of this decision are overwhelming. The loss of jobs, income and production is enormous. No less clear, on reflection, are the human and community consequences of these losses—the strains on marriage and family life, increased depression, alcoholism and alienation, as well as lost confidence, ambition and self-respect. It is especially hard on older workers who have given this company many years of service and who will find it exceedingly difficult to obtain new jobs. It exacerbates an already serious unemployment problem. It also threatens related industries and businesses as well as the tax base of several of our communities. This closing has already contributed to greater distrust and antagonism between various elements in our community. Behind the statistics and headlines lie individuals, families and communities left vulnerable and fearful by this decision. This is not in any sense a purely economic problem.

What happened on September 19 is clear. A compa-ny shut down a steel works and began laying off 5,000 workers. There are many explanations (of) why it happened. Some say that a conglomerate in deep financial trouble, faced with large capital costs for modernization and environmental protection, shut down an unprofitable steel mill. Others say that poor management, declining product quality, inadequate investment and absentee ownership resulted in a decision to close the mill. Still others believe that the steel industry has embarked on a strategy of concentration and reducing productive capacity in order to take full economic advantage of steel needs in the future and make the industry more profitable. Other analysts suggest that our present crisis is not simply the result of individual action. It is also a reflection of broader forces which have contributed to a significant loss of jobs in our region and the decline of tool, basic metals and other manufacturing. Our problems have been intensified by patterns of investment and relationships between capital and labor which have favored other regions and industries above our own. We suspect that each of these explanations contains some elements of truth. We know that each of them raises serious moral issues.

Moral Dimensions of the Crisis

What is the religious dimension of this? Why have we, as local representatives of the Catholic, Protestant, Jewish and Orthodox faiths, decided to issue this message and embark on a program of education and action to deal with this crisis? We enter this complex and controversial situation out of a concern for the victims of the shutdown, out of love for our Valley at a time of crisis and out of a conviction that religious faith provides essential insights for our problems and possible remedies.

Within the religious community, we are blessed with a rich resource in dealing with issues of economic and social life. The Scriptures point to important values which form our response: God's concern with the liberation of His people, the importance of work and stewardship. Our God is a God of justice. "The Lord, who does what is right, is always on the side of the oppressed." (Ps. 103:6) His message is very direct: "Cease to do evil. Learn to do good. Search for justice. Help the oppressed." (Isaiah 1:16-17) For those who are Christians, the life and ministry of Jesus lead us to similar concerns. Jesus came "to bring good news to the poor, to proclaim liberty to captives and new sight to the blind and to set the downtrodden free." (Luke 4:18) He very clearly identifies himself with the poor and the victims of injustice. "Whenever you did it for one of these, the least of my brothers, you did it for me." (Matt. 25:40) Our common religious tradition summons us to respond to our neighbors' needs and to work for justice.

In addition, our Judeo-Christian tradition has articulated a highly developed social teaching with direct relevance to issues of economic justice. This tradition insists that economic life ought to reflect the values of justice and respect for human dignity. The purpose of economic life is to serve the common good and the needs of people. This tradition also emphasizes the dignity of the human person and identifies those basic human rights which demand to be respected. These rights include the right to useful employment and to decent wages and income, the right to participation in economic decisions and even ownership, the right to bargain collectively, among others. These rights carry with them the responsibility to labor honestly and productively for the common good. These corollary responsibilities apply to employee and employer alike. Our social teachings further lead us to the conviction that government is required to preserve and defend human rights when private action fails to insure them. Economic institutions, although they have their own purposes and methods, still must serve the common good and are subject to moral judgment. We are convinced, in short, that corporations have social and moral responsibilities.

We believe that the performance of the Lykes Corporation, in this instance, fails to meet this fundamental moral criterion. We say this not to condemn individuals, but to examine a system in which persons feel compelled to make such harsh decisions and to do so in secrecy. We believe that industrial investment decisions ought to take into account the needs and desires of employees and the community at large. In its refusal to invest in new equipment or necessary maintenance, the Lykes Corporation failed to do this. Human beings and community life are higher values than corporate profits. In its decision to close the steel works, we believe that the Lykes Corporation followed a different course. Our common faiths teach us the value of stewardship of material and human resources. We believe that the Lykes Corporation failed the test of stewardship in the management of this company and its resources.

Our traditional teaching points out that economic decisions ought not to be left to the judgment of a few persons with economic power, but should be shared with the larger community which is affected by the decisions. In the suddenness, the totality and the secrecy of this decision, the Lykes Corporation ignored this principle. Corporations have a social responsibility to their employees and to the community, as well as a responsibility to shareholders. By their abandonment of Youngstown, the Lykes Corporation has neglected this corporate social responsibility. We deplore not only the decision to close the steel mill, but also the manner in which the decision was made, the way it is being implemented, and the pattern of neglect which led to it.

At the same time, the Lykes Corporation does not bear the sole responsibility for this crisis. Local, national and international forces are at work which created the environment for such actions. Locally, a preoccupation with our own individual interests and a lack of concern for our common good may have contributed to our present problem. It is possible, for example, that an excessive concern with higher and higher wages and better and better fringe benefits may have contributed to the situation which now confronts us. We wonder whether labor and management have worked together as well as they could to solve their common problems. Perhaps production costs have been raised by the failure of railroads to overcome their jurisdictional and territorial conflicts as well as work regulations which make efficient and direct transportation of steel and raw materials impossible. Nationally, the failure to formulate a comprehensive national policy to retain and support the manufacture of basic steel is a serious failing which helped to bring about our present state. Internationally, the willingness of some foreign steel producers to "dump" steel at below market prices into the United States has contributed to our difficulties.

However, our response to this crisis cannot be based on a search for scapegoats. We should not permit the evasion of responsibility by those whose decisions and policies primarily created this situation. We were disturbed by the Lykes Corporation's attempt to focus responsibility for their action upon environmental laws, imported steel and governmental efforts to keep down the cost of steel. While these factors may have contributed to this decision, it is worth noting that the amount of steel imported into the United States has remained relatively constant for the past ten years. We also understand that industry expenditures on pollution abatement equipment as a percentage of total capital expenditures have remained relatively constant to the price index. We say this not to minimize these problems, but to point out that other factors may also be responsible for the decision.

A Response to the Crisis

The religious community has a responsibility to address this crisis, the suffering it entails, and the attitudes and forces which created it. We are faced with a choice between resignation and despair or firm acceptance of our responsibility to act in accordance with our beliefs. Our situation in Youngstown is an opportunity as well as a serious problem. It is an opportunity to give witness to our religious principles of justice, to alleviate pain, and to create new models of concern and involvement. For this reason, representatives of various religious congregations in the Mahoning Valley have been meeting to formulate a creative and focused response. This common message is a first product of our ongoing collaboration.

In the face of this crisis, we need unity, common purpose and coordinated action for the good of the community. Time is short. We in the religious community attempt to respond to this crisis with no vested interest or hidden concerns other than the welfare of our community. It is our intention to provide a common ground and an impetus for community efforts without substituting for other legitimate interests. We do not wish to take the place of leaders of industry, union leaders, business representatives and government officials. Rather, we seek to avoid political rivalry and organizational conflict. Motivated by pastoral concern, we wish to raise issues, serve our community and call upon these and other groups to play their essential roles in restoring and rebuilding the economic vitality of our Valley.

We wish to cooperate with other groups and individuals seeking remedies to this crisis. We are eager to join our efforts to those of workers and their unions, political officials, responsible business and corporate leaders, and other members of the Mahoning Valley seeking to restore the economic health of our community.

First, we will initiate programs of education. We will seek to continue to raise the moral and human dimensions of this crisis, clarify the causes of our problems and emphasize the need for diversification in our regional economy. We will also attempt to help national leaders and organizations understand the dimensions of our crisis and the national and international forces which contribute to it. We will work with the national religious community to develop programs which emphasize corporate responsibility and the relationship between economic decisions and social justice. What we do in this area could serve as a focus for national education and action within the religious community.

In this context, it is important to remind ourselves that our problems are not unique. Recently, some 20,000 steelworkers across the country have lost their jobs as a result of plant closings. In our nation, nearly seven million people are out of work, according to government statistics. Millions more have given up looking for work out of frustration. In parts of our own area, unemployment is a way of life rather than a recent threat. In our concern for the victims of recent layoffs, we cannot neglect the critical problems of those who are unemployed because of discrimination, lack of skills, lack of mobility, or simply a lack of jobs. As we fashion a specific response to this particular shutdown, we also commit ourselves to the ongoing and related struggles for full employment and equal opportunity for all people. Our current distress should strengthen the resolve of each of us to work toward an economy which provides a job for every person able and willing to work.

Secondly, we will seek short- and long-term remedies to the crisis and its consequences. We strongly support efforts to aid laid-off workers and their families in coping with the economic, social and emotional trauma of joblessness. We will seek to intensify social service efforts in our own institutions and to deploy them in new ways to meet the enormous needs of the victims of the shutdown.

More significantly, we are prepared to assist, in whatever way we can, the efforts to save the jobs of the workers affected by the shutdown. The skilled steelworkers of the Valley and the facilities of the mill, despite its age, constitute major resources for the region and the nation. To allow the workers to scatter and to stand by and watch the mill deteriorate further would be a tragic waste. We fully support proposals for interim maintenance of the Campbell works. In addition, we have begun a process of seriously exploring the possibility of community and/or worker ownership of the Sheet and Tube plant or other positive alternative use of the facilities to employ the workers. We have decided to help fund a feasibility study to examine the potential purchase and operation of the facilities by workers and/or the community. In pledging our support of such efforts, we recognize that this would be a serious undertaking. However, the idea of worker and community ownership is not foreign to our religious and national traditions. It ought to be explored as a creative response to abandonment of the mill by outside interests.

We also call upon other major employers in the Valley, especially other steel companies, to pledge publicly, community and employee consultation in future economic and investment decisions affecting employment and community life. The failure of Lykes to share its problems and options with the community and its abrupt decison to shut down cannot be repeated. We will seek these pledges as a good faith gesture on the part of the industrial and investment community. We believe that they would contribute to a significant reduction in anxiety and distrust.

The decision of the Lykes Corporation to close its Sheet and Tube operation does not terminate the Corporation's responsibility to the Mahoning Valley, even though merger or other alternatives are being discussed. Litigation against the company is being contemplated by other organizations and individuals. In addition, we hope that Lykes will fully cooperate with the efforts of those seeking to provide minimal maintenance for the mill and those exploring the feasibility of operation under different auspices. In particular, we believe that Lykes has a moral responsibility to respond generously to a genuine and realistic program to reopen the mill under community, worker or public ownership. In setting a price for the purchase of the mill and in cooperating with potential new managers, Lykes has an obligation to assist in efforts to repair the extensive damage which has come from its decision to close the mill.

Thirdly, we in the religious community will join with others to advocate an effective national policy to retain in our region, basic steel and the jobs related to it. This will include administrative and legislative action to:

• provide federal aid for modernization of existing steel facilities in severely impacted areas where steelworkers already live.

• (adopt) government purchasing policies which provide preferential treatment for mills and communities in deep financial trouble.

• encourage increased use of steel to meet human and community needs.

• seek changes in economic policies which unfairly pit region against region for jobs and economic growth, encourage the development of conglomerates and neglect the needs of older and urban communities.

We will join with others in advocating new policies and greater urgency in responding to the deterioration of our steel-making capability. We will meet with officials of the Carter Administration and the Congress, as well as leaders of state and local government, industry and labor, and point out the human and community dimensions of the crisis and the need for prompt and compassionate action to relieve our distress. We believe that Youngstown can serve as a model for cooperative action and governmental aid to assist workers and the community to save jobs and economic strength. In the past the federal government has acted to provide large-scale assistance to private corporations in financial difficulties. Clearly, the needs of our community are at least as compelling and worthy of a response. In fact, we believe that this situation offers an even greater opportunity to renew and revitalize the confidence and productive capacity of an entire community. It is our profound hope that the federal government will join in partnership with our community to fashion a new road to economic health and well-being for the Mahoning Valley—and to do so in a manner which can suggest new directions for other communities as well.

We call upon the members of our community to join together in a comprehensive plan of action to develop the will, the resources and the commitment to revitalize our Valley. This effort will require the cooperation of every sector of Youngstown: churches, synagogues, labor, business, financial institutions, government, and other organizations and individuals. In this common effort, we can rebuild far more than our economic capacity, we can renew the ties of common purpose and concern which can help us to become a better and more just community. This will not be easy, but the suffering of our people, the precarious position of our Valley, the teaching of our faith and the ideals of our nation require a determined effort to respond to this crisis.

These educational, economic development and advocacy efforts must be accompanied by our constant prayers and vivid recollection of the realities of hope, regeneration and redemption. As religious people, we have ample cause for hope even in the midst of suffering. By our concern, by our application of religious principles to this crisis, and by our commitment to action, we are carrying on the Judeo-Christian tradition which is "to do justice, to love mercy and to walk humbly with God." (Micah 6:8) In so doing, we discover the basic hope. As the Prophet Isaiah said:

> Look, you do business on your fastdays,
> you oppress all your workmen and strike the
> poor man with your fist...
> let the oppressed go free,
> and break every yoke,
> share your bread with the hungry
> and shelter the homeless poor,
> clothe the man you see to be naked
> and not turn from your own kin?
> Then will your light shine like the dawn
> and your wound be quickly healed over . . .

If you do away with the yoke,
the clenched fist, the wicked word,
if you give your bread to the hungry,
and relief to the oppressed,
your light will rise in the darkness,
and your shadows become like noon.
You will rebuild the ancient ruins,
build up on the old foundations.
You will be called "Conciliator,
restorer of households." (Isaiah 58, *Jerusalem Bible*)

Questions for Reflection

The following questions were circulated to people in the Mahoning Valley in Ohio. How would you answer them:

1. The statement suggests that the action of the Lykes Corporation on September 19th raises "profound issues of corporate responsibility and justice." What is corporate responsibility? What are some of the issues that come to mind?

2. Do you think that persons within the Lykes Corporation, primarily responsible for the September 19th decision, were informed by religious teaching? If so, in what way and, if not, why?

3. Corporations may have social and moral responsibilities, but should not a church or synagogue concern itself with its central task of worship and nurture and refrain from entering the political-economic world?

4. Do you believe it is possible and/or desirable to let economic decisions be made by those who are affected by them? Why?

Exercises for Reflection

1. Relate the above questions to Articles 6 & 7 of the International Covenant on Economic, Social and Cultural Rights (printed at the beginning of this chapter). What responsibility does the government of the United States or Canada have towards implementing these rights? How do these governments deal with the right to work, and the right to just and favorable conditions of work? What is the relationship of governments to corporations such as the Lykes Corporation? What should the relationship be?

2. The following questions were also asked people in the Mahoning Valley. However, to answer them you will need to try to imagine it is your own community which has been affected. Imagine that an Ecumenical Coalition was organized in your community and would ask these questions. First of all, who would participate in this Ecumenical Coalition? What would

be your major economic institution or institutions which might make the same decision the Lykes Corporation made? How would your community be affected?

a. What are some of the obstacles that you can see as the Ecumenical Coalition attempts to organize (in the Valley, known for its wide ethnic diversity of peoples and culture)?

b. Assuming that there is a chance for the development of a new enterprise that would re-employ the (5,000) persons laid off by the (Lykes) decision, name the ten persons and/or groups that you think would be most likely, locally, to bring this about.

c. As you look at the list you have just comprised in b, what does it say to you about whom you trust? Have you ever directly benefited from any of the persons and/or groups that you have listed? Have you ever been injured by any of the persons and/or groups that you listed?

d. Do you believe that the (Lykes) decision—the manner in which it was made—will tend to make other (steel) companies (in the Valley) more or less willing to confide in the public with respect to their economic plans (in the Valley)? Why?

e. As a resident (of the Valley), do you think that there is anything that you can do to contribute toward a solution of the problem created by the (Lykes) decision of (September 19th)? What religious understandings inform your response?

(Parentheses have been placed around those parts of the questions which you should replace with what would be appropriate in your community.)

Preparing for Effective Witness: Further Reading

"At the United Nations," Chapter 1, pp. 21-30 in *Paradox and Promise in Human Rights* by Peggy Billings.

"The Critique of the Covenant: The Social Contract Broken and Renewed," Chapter 11, pp. 75-83 in *The Liberating Bond...* by Wolfgang Roth and Rosemary Radford Ruether.

Resources

Ecumenical Coalition of the Mahoning Valley, 263 Federal Plaza West, Youngstown, Ohio 44503.

Save Youngstown: Save America: JSAC Grapevine, Vol. 9, #6, January 1978. Available from Grapevine, Room 1700-A, 475 Riverside Drive, New York, New York 10027.

"The Fight Against Black Monday" — 27 minutes/ color. The film describes how ever since the Lykes

Corporation, a New Orleans based conglomerate, bought the plant in 1963 they had taken profits out of the area, but made little new investment to maintain machinery or modernize the facility. The problem is not unique to Youngstown; across the industrial heart-land of the Northeast, plants are systematically "milked" before entire industries are moved to the Sunbelt or the developing world.

But Youngstown's response was unique and leader-ship came from an unexpected source—an ecumeni-cal coalition of over 200 local clergymen. Father Edward Stanton, Coordinator of the Ecumenical Co-alition, explains the churches' new involvement in economic issues: "We have to question the morality of any act that affects whole communities adversely. Pastorally, we heard five thousand guys saying, we want our jobs back."

Produced by ABC Television, 1978, available from California Newsreel, 630 Natoma, San Francisco, California 94103. Rental: $40. Also available from McGraw-Hill Company, Film Division, 1221 Avenue of the Americas, New York, New York 10020. Rental: $35.

"Temiscaming," about a U.S.-owned paper compa-ny closing a local pulp mill in the small Quebec town of Temiscaming. A consortium of a pulpworkers union, the provincial government, and Canadian busi-nessmen was able to reopen the mill. Their problems are not over. Labor-management antagonisms contin-ue and the film raises questions about potential of co-ownership without democratic management with worker participation at all levels of decision-making. Produced by National Film Board of Canada, Box 6100, Station A, Montreal PQ, Canada H3C 3H5. (Canadians should check for a local Film Board distribution—no cost for rental.) Also available from California Newsreel (see address above), 64 minutes /color. Rental: $70.

"Why Work?" Parts 1 & 2—30 minutes each part/color. In part 1, the nature, value and outcome of work for people around the world are explored. In part 2, personal testimonies from workers and re-searchers reveal the detrimental effects of unemploy-ment on mental and physical health. Produced by WNET—Bill Moyer's Journal, 1976. Available from California Newsreel (address shown above). Rental: $45 a part; $80 for both parts.

"On the Line"—A very human portrayal of the struggle of people in the U.S. to control their own lives...The appeal of the film is in the optimism and community which they find through their struggle. 16

mm., color, 50 minutes. Available from Latin America Film Project, P.O. Box 315, Franklin Lakes, NJ 07417. Rental: $75.

CHAPTER 8
TO SECURE A CORRECTION OF ABUSES
A STATEMENT BY RELIGIOUS LEADERS

Article 8

1. The States Parties to the present Covenant undertake to ensure:

(a) The right of everyone *to form trade unions and join the trade union* of his (her) choice, subject only to the rules of the organization concerned, for the promotion and protection of his (her) economic and social interests. No restrictions may be placed on the exercise of the right other than those prescribed by law and which are necessary in a democratic society in the *interests of national security or public order* or for the protection of the rights and freedoms of others;

(b) The right of trade unions to establish national federations or confederations and the right of the latter to form or join international trade-union organizations;

(c) The right of trade unions to function freely subject to no limitations other than those prescribed by law and which are necessary in a democratic society in the interests of national security or public order or for the protection of the rights and freedoms of others;

(d) The right to strike, provided that it is exercised in conformity with the laws of the particular country.

2. This article shall not prevent the imposition of lawful restrictions on the exercise of these rights by members of the armed forces or of the police or of the administration of the State.

3. Nothing in this article shall authorize States Parties to the International Labour Organisation Convention of 1948 concerning Freedom of Association and Protection of the Right to Organize to take legislative measures which would prejudice, or apply the law in such a manner as would prejudice, the guarantees provided for in that Convention.

International Covenant on Economic,
Social and Cultural Rights (Italics added)

In a country where the freedom to form and join trade unions has a long tradition, the struggle has a long way to go. One of the current cases is the right of the J.P. Stevens workers to organize and engage in collective bargaining. For several years now the dispute has been raging throughout the many plants of the J.P. Stevens Company. The religious community in the U.S.A. joined the efforts to "secure a correction of abuses in faithfulness to the gospel." On April 19, 1978, an Interfaith Delegation, meeting with the workers in Montgomery, Alabama, issued the following statement:

In the Judeo-Christian tradition, love is expressed in society by the establishment of justice. Where injustice is found to exist, religious groups must make vigorous efforts to secure a correction of abuses, in faithfulness to the gospel.

The current struggle of J.P. Stevens' workers for industrial justice is more than a labor-management dispute. J.P. Stevens has escalated the workers' attempts to organize into a major question of social justice for American society. It has refused to follow the normal legal procedures our nation has developed to produce approximate justice between workers and management. Both the Federal District Court and the

National Labor Relations Board have found the company guilty of refusal to bargain in good faith with the union. J.P. Stevens has also been convicted of illegal firings of workers, harassment and intimidation of union supporters and other illegal acts. By so doing, the Company has challenged the whole balance of interests and powers that has been developed to insure the rights of all persons in an industrial private enterprise economy.

The workers of the J.P. Stevens plant in Montgomery, Alabama, are attempting to organize their plant. In order to increase awareness regarding their efforts, they invited representatives of religious groups which have nationally endorsed the J.P. Stevens campaign to Montgomery.

Today, in response to their invitation, we have learned first hand that the abuses documented in the court records are continuing. We have heard about harassment on the job because of union activity, unsafe and hazardous working conditions, arbitrary and capricious changing of job assignments, lack of adequate health, accident and retirement benefits. Apparently, J.P. Stevens is willing to accept public welfare money to supplement their workers' incomes, instead of providing adequate wages and pensions. Workers conveyed to us the oppressive atmosphere toward pro-union employees present inside the plant.

We sought an opportunity to meet with the local management at their plant, but they refused.

Traditionally, religious groups have relied upon moral suasion to correct injustice. But moral suasion has proven singularly ineffective with the management of J.P. Stevens. Therefore, the time has come when moral suasion must be coupled with direct action.

We commit ourselves to increased efforts to communicate the news of the boycott of J.P. Stevens products to our churches and memberships, and to enlist their support.

We commit ourselves to continue close attention to the workers in J.P. Stevens plants throughout the nation.

We call upon all responsible employees in the Montgomery area to provide employment for workers who have been fired for union activity by J.P. Stevens.

We call upon regional and state religious bodies to join us in support of the boycott of J.P. Stevens products.

We call for the establishment of a national interfaith committee to support the boycott of J.P. Stevens products.

We call upon all people of good faith to support the rights of J.P. Stevens workers by supporting a national consumers' boycott of the Company's products.

We call upon all people of good faith to contact their Senators to support the Labor Law Reform Bill (S. 1883) now before the U.S. Senate, which strengthens the ability of the National Labor Relations Board to achieve its original purposes.

Dr. George Outen, General Secretary
Board of Church and Society
United Methodist Church

Dr. Howard Spragg, Executive Vice President
United Church Board for Homeland Ministries
United Church of Christ

Dr. Kenneth Kuntz, President
Division of Homeland Ministries
Christian Church (Disciples of Christ)

Sister Kathleen Keating, Chairperson
National Assembly of Women Religious

Father Jim Ratigan, President
National Federation of Priests' Councils

Ms. Ruth Gilbert, Secretary for Community Action
The Women's Division
United Methodist Church

Rev. Sally AsKew, National Board Member
Women's Division
United Methodist Church

Rev. James Sessions, Executive Director
Southerners for Economic Justice

Questions for Reflection

1. Summarize the position adopted by the church leaders in this statement. What is your denomination's stand on labor-management relations, on collective bargaining? What is your position? Why?

2. Does an "industrial private enterprise economy" assume that labor and management have the same rights? What in fact is meant by a "balance of interests and powers"? Describe what your understanding of the economic system is. What rights do workers have? What rights does management have?

3. Does the nature of human rights differ according to the position held within the "industrial private enterprise economy"?

4. What bearing does the nature of the economic system have on human rights?

5. Has the right to form a trade union always been

respected in the United States or Canada? If not, who has prevented this right? How?

6. What other examples do you know where workers have been prevented from belonging to a trade union, or from forming a trade union? What is the situation for Africans in South Africa (see Chapter 3)?

Exercises for Reflection

In the statement the religious leaders say: "In the Judeo-Christian tradition, love is expressed in society by the establishment of justice. Where injustice is found to exist, religious groups must make vigorous efforts to secure a correction of abuses, in faithfulness to the gospel."

Do you agree? How does this relate to Dwain Epps' statement, "It is the task of the church, in defense of human rights, to lend support to these political efforts without which real guarantees for human rights are but illusions." (Introduction to Section II)

Does the church need to be involved in political action "to secure a correction of abuses"? How do the religious leaders answer this question? Explain your feelings about their action.

Preparing for Effective Witness: Further Reading

"To Restore the Economic Health of the Community," Chapter 7.

"At the United Nations," Chapter 1, pp. 21-30 in *Paradox and Promise in Human Rights* by Peggy Billings.

"The Critique of the Covenant: The Social Contract Broken and Renewed," Chapter 11, pp. 75-83 of *The Liberating Bond . . .* by Wolfgang Roth and Rosemary Radford Ruether. Particular attention should be given to the Social Gospel Movement, p. 81.

Resources

Fabric of Injustice: The Struggle at J.P. Stevens (1978), a pamphlet put out by the National Council of Churches of Christ in the USA. Available from: Economic Justice, NCC, Room 572, 475 Riverside Drive, New York, New York 10027. Single copies: 30¢ each (includes postage); bulk (10 or more), 20¢ each (plus postage).

Straightening Things Out (1977), a pamphlet put out by J.P. Stevens & Co. Inc., 1185 Avenue of the Americas, New York, New York 10036. Since the NCC pamphlet was published later, you might wish to ask for up-to-date information from the company.

"Justice vs. J.P. Stevens," a film available from the Amalgamated Clothing Textile Workers Union, 111 15th Street, New York, New York 10003.

"Harlan County, U.S.A."—a documentary about striking miners in Kentucky in 1974. Interviews with active members of the long strike as well as leaders of the corporation that owns the mines. Depicts the strong confrontation between the two groups, and the poor lives of the miners. 103 minutes. Available from Cinema 5, 595 Madison Avenue, New York, New York 10022. Rental: $150 if no admission charges; $200 if admission.

"We Just Won't Take It"—On October 15, 1975, the Canadian Government introduced wage controls. The labor movement saw that this program attacked one of the few instruments working people have for defending themselves in an unequal society—collective bargaining through their unions. This film is a documentary on the struggle of the workers to express their opposition to the controls. Produced by UAW/Jim Littleton, Canada, 1976, 55 minutes, color. Available from DEC Films, 121 Avenue Road, Toronto M5R 2G3.

"Stand Together"—In August 1976 a small group of minority women, mainly Asians and West Indians, formed a union and were fired from a North London Film Processing Factory called Grunwick. Immediately following the dismissal they protested in front of the factory. This was the beginning of a long, bitter struggle for the reassessment of their rights, and for union recognition and reinstatement in the company. Produced by London Newsreel Collective, 52 minutes /color, 1977. Available from California Newsreel, 630 Natoma, San Francisco, California 94103. Rental: $75.

CHAPTER 9
TO PROMOTE THE GENERAL WELFARE
BY EARLY CHILDHOOD PROJECT — COLORADO
THE CARNEGIE COUNCIL ON CHILDREN — NEW YORK
THE COALITION FOR CHILDREN & YOUTH —
WASHINGTON, D. C.*

Article 10

The States Parties to the present Covenant recognize that:

1. The *widest possible protection and assistance should be accorded to the family, which is the natural and fundamental group unit of society,* particularly for its establishment and while it is responsible for the care and education of dependent children. Marriage must be entered into with the free consent of the intending spouses.

2. Special protection should be accorded to mothers during a reasonable period before and after childbirth. During such period working mothers should be accorded paid leave or leave with adequate social security benefits.

3. Special measures of protection and assistance should be taken on behalf of all children and young persons without any discrimination for reasons of parentage or other conditions. Children and young persons should be protected from economic and social exploitation. Their employment in work harmful to their morals or health or dangerous to life or likely to hamper their normal development should be punishable by law. States should also set age limits below which the paid employment of child labour should be prohibited and punishable by law.

International Covenant on Economic,
Social and Cultural Rights (Italics added)

Article 23

1. *The family is the natural and fundamental group unit of society and is entitled to protection by society and the State.*

2. The right of men and women of marriageable age *to marry and to found a family* shall be recognized.

3. No marriage shall be entered into without the *free and full consent* of the intending spouses.

4. States Parties to the present Covenant shall take appropriate steps to ensure *equality of rights and responsibilities of spouses as to marriage, during marriage and at its dissolution.* In the case of dissolution, provision shall be made for the necessary protection of any children.

International Covenant on Civil and
Political Rights (Italics added)

David Gilbankian comes from a seemingly serene middle-class home. His father is a high official in the federal government. His mother does not work for pay but is active in church and community activities. David, 16, has one brother in college and another age 12.

He has become involved in regular and heavy drug and alcohol use, has been truant from school more often than not, and was recently suspended from school for fighting.

His parents no longer have any ideas about what to do with him. He refuses to listen, will not tell them where he gets the money for drugs or where he goes when he is not home. They are afraid he may get arrested but are beginning to think that might actually be good for him and them.

Helen Baker separated from her husband when he started drinking heavily and hitting the children. She took a blue collar job at an auto assembly plant putting bumpers on a conveyor belt. She doesn't like the work much but it pays better than a clerical job and enough to afford a babysitter for her two children, ages two and three. She makes $250 a week on the job and pays $50 a week for the two children for all-day care in a neighbor's house. Because the children do nothing but sit around all day and watch television, she would prefer to have them in a more professional day-care program.

Sarah Stolka is a junior in high school. She wants to get contraceptive information, but her school has no sex education classes and she is uncertain whether she can find a clinic downtown that will help without her mother's permission. She wants some place she can take her friend Ann, as well, who says she doesn't care about contraception and wants to get pregnant so that she can have a baby of her own.

Hank Maguire has a job selling highly technical medical equipment for a large company, which he enjoys and is good at, but which keeps him out of town a good deal. His wife has apparently recovered from a nervous breakdown she suffered several years ago, but is showing some of the same signs of strain that marked her last illness. Their four children are now in elementary and high school. Mr. Maguire wants some temporary homemaking help for his family, and would like a personal counseling support for his wife apart from the large impersonal hospital setting where she went before. Neither service seems

to be available for families in his upper-middle-income bracket. He has approached his company about a temporary leave of absence for himself, but they insist that they need him on a number of new negotiations.

Judy Lieberman has two young children. Her husband recently divorced her, and has left town without leaving his address; he has stopped sending the child support payments which helped her make ends meet in the first year of their divorce. She would like to move back to Cincinnati, where her parents live, so that she could provide a better family atmosphere for her children and take advantage of her mother's offer to help with child care. That would mean leaving the bank teller job she has now, and her reasonably priced apartment. She needs help in locating new housing, a new job, a new health care arrangement for her family, and advice about day care or pre-school for the older child.

Bill and his sister June have had a tough childhood. Their father left them after June was born and their mother started working as a waitress and bringing home men to earn extra money. Their mother's drinking increased and she started "acting crazy." She was committed to the state mental hospital when Bill was 12 and his sister was 11. When their mother was committed, the county placed them in a foster home. The foster home was, according to the two, "O.K." but they stayed there only for a year because their foster parents decided to move out of the state. Two more homes in six months and then their mother was released from the hospital. They re-established a home of their own, but it only lasted for 18 months until their mother went into the mental hospital again. Both were then teenagers. The county took charge of them for the next three years, but could not find a home that would take both Bill and his sister—so they were split up. Before his 18th birthday, Bill had lived in four different foster homes. He was "troubled" in each.

Services—we all get them and use them. In fact, the "services" sector of the economy is growing faster than any other. When we go out to eat we are getting a service. When the typewriter repairman comes to the office he is performing a service. We pick a restaurant because we have heard about it, read an advertisement for it, or someone we know recommends it. We can find a repairman through the same avenues or by looking in the yellow pages.

But the services needed by the families in our examples are not obtained as simply as getting a meal served or a typewriter repaired. They require dealing

*Chapter 5 of *The Children's Political Checklist*, Report #103, September 1977, Early Childhood Project, The Carnegie Foundation on Children, New York City. Used by permission.

with government or private agencies and, possibly, law enforcement officials or other public officials/agencies. They involve very personal problems that are not always easy to share with a stranger.

We take it as a matter of course that government will provide such basic services as education, or fire and police protection, or public health inspections. And we take it as a matter of course that the federal government will provide for the national defense, conduct a census, and do those things prescribed by the Constitution. But the Constitution has only general language about promoting the general welfare, and each generation of Americans must evaluate what that means in terms of public support for social needs.

After a period of great growth in government attempts to ameliorate social problems in the 1960s, and then a time of disillusionment about the effectiveness of government programs, many people now seem to be looking for new and better approaches to solving social problems.

Of course, it sometimes appears that people are willing to reduce only those programs that they themselves do not benefit from. For example, most people do not regard the tax deduction taken for the interest they pay on their home mortgage as either a "loophole" or a subsidy by the federal government to them to encourage single family home ownership. Yet many people regard a federal program of building public housing or paying rent subsidies to the poor as an unnecessary federal expenditure. In short, homeowners are willing to accept federal assistance in meeting their own housing costs, but are not willing to see their tax dollars spent to assist others (those who cannot afford to buy their own homes) with their housing costs.

The families described at the beginning of this chapter have very serious problems: children at odds with their parents, children abandoned by their parents, parents too overwhelmed by the stress of poverty to organize the kind of upbringing for their children that they know is best, parents who in spite of having money to pay for helpful services can't find what they need. Thus, the delicate question of the proper relationship between families and government adds an important and difficult dimension to the related problem of how much subsidy of public services the government can afford with our tax money. With the provision of social services often comes the power of public officials or professional care-takers to make important decisions about the future of children.

Traditionally in America many family services have been provided by private voluntary organizations on a charitable basis. In recent years, more and more public agencies have begun to play a part in legal services to families, in the care of mistreated children, in adoption proceedings, in mental health programs, in family planning services, in day care, in temporary homemaking, and even in family counseling. Both the National Academy of Sciences Committee and the Carnegie Council on Children took a long look at the present fragmented and inadequate combination of public and private social services and came to the conclusion that fundamental changes and coordination are necessary.

This promises to be a tremendous job. Many social services are now provided by institutions and people that clearly have a stake in continuing what they consider to be an important function. Every consumer has a bright idea about how to improve a program each knows about. Reformers want scope to experiment with new ideas and ways to deliver better services. Child and family welfare programs now constitute a very big industry, encompassing a wide range of philosophical differences.

Both the National Academy of Sciences Committee and the Carnegie Council have concluded that the way to get a handle on this problem is to begin at the local level, by reinforcing the power of parents and consumers to organize services, and by integrating family services into a more coherent and usable network. The National Academy of Sciences Committee recommends neighborhood resource centers which would be able to:

• respond to the needs of families by integrating and coordinating a wide range of existing programs as well as providing new services if they are needed. Each center would also undertake a continual assessment of such needs. The primary focus would be on those families designated as being at high risk, although services would be provided to other families on a fee basis.

• Centers would not attempt to provide all services on site (for example, complete health care) but rather, would assist in meeting family needs and obtaining services to which families are entitled by providing ombudsman and advocacy services to insure effective follow through. In addition, community resource specialists on the staff of each center would devote their principal attention to mobilizing existing community resources—schools, private industry, public agencies —to support families.

The Carnegie Council on Children supports such an

integration of service functions, and also suggests the formation of "consumers councils", with a heavy representation of parents to gather information about child and family needs, and "audit" the performance of the providers. They also suggest that strong grievance mechanisms be built into the system to insure that clients have a place to turn with their complaints.

In every community there are many children and parents with large and small problems. Some capture public attention when a case of child abuse appears on the front page, or when a facility to house runaway teenagers is raided by a narcotics squad. Some are simply familiar to all of us who have had a neighbor or family member come seeking advice about finding a suitable day-care arrangement, or about whether to help a teenage daughter find contraceptive advice, or about how to find a marriage counselor—or a divorce lawyer. The list of questions which follows illuminates assumptions underlying the public and private network of services which we all use, or might one day use. The answers to these questions would provide the framework within which a better social service system could be built.

Questions for Reflection

1. What social services does your town, county, state, provide? Is there a place in the neighborhood where people can get information about what programs are available to them? Can they get help to establish their eligibility, or to fill out forms?

2. Are family services open to all? Are they restricted to people of a certain income? Neighborhood? Religion? Age?

3. Are there different kinds of services provided by public agencies, so that families can choose the one that best suits their needs? For example, all-day center day care, and small family home units, and morning-only or afternoon-only possibilities? Day care with a high educational component and day care that concentrates on rest and recreation?

4. Do social service agencies tend to separate families in order to "solve" problems, without examining alternatives? How many children are placed in foster care or institutional care during crises that might better be resolved by providing support to the family itself? Do family members have to go to hospitals for physical or mental treatment, because that is how insurance coverage is available, even though they could more appropriately and inexpensively be helped at home?

5. How many people use the services that are available? How many are eligible? Is there any outreach effort? Does the service provide for secondary services such as transportation or babysitting? Are the services open before or after regular working hours? Are there long waiting lines, or waiting lists for appointments?

6. How are services paid for? If they are privately run, or government provided, is there a sliding scale of fees according to income? Is the test to determine someone's income reasonably administered? If low-income people can use the program without cost, is there a "notch" which means such people lose their access to the facility for just a small increase in income?

7. Are facilities used by a mix of different kinds of people? Should they be? Would that affect the quality of services provided? Would it affect the feeling people have about their own family life and problems?

8. Who runs the programs? If they are paid for by private funds, is there a community board? If they are public programs, who sets standards, does the hiring of personnel, evaluates the program? Is there provision for consumer or parent participation in running the service? How do program administrators find out what the clients think about the program?

9. Is there an ombudsman or complaint center where complaints against government services can be registered?

Exercises for Reflection

The major question raised in this chapter is regarding the role of government in relationship to families:

a. Discuss the role government should have.

b. Discuss the implications for the role of government in light of Article 10 of the International Covenant on Economic, Social and Cultural Rights and Article 23 of the International Covenant on Civil and Political Rights (reread them at the beginning of this chapter).

c. Discuss the role that private voluntary organizations, which include the church, play in relation to families. Should they continue, or is there another role for them today?

Early in the seventies the Christian Council of Bombay, India, faced some of the same issues. In 1973 this group issued a practical proposal titled, *The Call to Justice and Peace*, which said in part:

> That we live in radical times is undisputed. The foundations of every social institution and individual are being uprooted by the emergence of a new urban, scientific and secular world. The mission of the

church as it has been expressed in recent history, through schools, hospitals, charitable organizations and evangelism is in serious question. One must assume that the particularities of the churches' social mission are gifts that have now been given to society. No longer are health care and education options to human existence. They have become essential to man throughout the globe. And it is the church that has been largely responsible for this concrete example of love of neighbour. That battle has been won and the contribution received.

Now, as in ages past, God is calling us to pioneer new fields of mission appropriate to his on-going creation. The magnitude of innocent suffering leaves no doubt as to his call to recreate the structures of love and the style of witnessing to the word of Jesus Christ. The mission of the church is on behalf of all mankind.

Illustrative of the implications of recreating "the structures of love and the style of witness to the word of Jesus Christ" are the words of Dr. M. M. Thomas:

> The change in the concept of service in recent years has been too radical for the church in Asia and has swept it off balance, so that it has yet to find its feet properly on the ground.
>
> Firstly, with non-Christian agencies, the neighbourhood communities and the state itself becoming awake to the increasing responsibility in education, health and other social services, there is a shift in emphasis from Christian institutions of service under Christian management to Christian participation in institutions of service run by others or in partnership with others. Even where Christian institutions have large room for service, the state as the organ of the whole community has increasing control.
>
> Secondly, Christian service in the past has concentrated on the service of charity and compassion to the poor, expressing itself in relief of the unjust social institutions. No doubt the "poor" will be with us in any society and the service of charity will continue to have its place. But there has been a shift from what Professor Takenaka calls "charitable diakonia" to "social diakonia," that is from social service to social action aimed at changing structures, institutions and laws of society. This has brought about the need of discriminating participation in power politics as a means of service.
>
> Thirdly, a growing technical society has brought about new social structures and new functional groups, all of them serving the needs of only fragments of man and none the whole man. This is so different from the services in a traditional structure which took care of the whole man, body, mind and soul at once.

("The Christian Response to the Asian Revolution" quoted in *The Call to Justice and Peace.*)

Can we in the United States and Canada identify with the Church in India? Could these same words describe our own dilemma?

Resources

All Our Children, The American Family Under Pressure, by Kenneth Keniston and the Carnegie Council on Children (New York and London: Harcourt, Brace, Jovanovich, 1977). A Harvest paperback edition is available and a bulk sale price is possible for *non-profit institutions.* 1-4 copies (20% off list—$3.16 per copy), 5-25 copies (25% off list—$2.96 per copy), 26 and over (40% off list—$2.37 per copy). Order from Institutional Marketing Department, Harcourt, Brace, Jovanovich, 757 Third Avenue, New York, N.Y. 10017.

CHAPTER 10
TO DEMOCRATIZE THE SYSTEM OF EDUCATION
CHIQUI A.S. VICIOSO

Article 13

1. The States Parties to the present Covenant recognize *the right of everyone to education*. They agree that education shall be directed to the full development of the human personality and the sense of its dignity, and shall strengthen the respect for human rights and fundamental freedoms. They further agree that education shall enable all persons to participate effectively in a free society, promote understanding, tolerance and friendship among all nations and all racial, ethnic or religious groups, and further the activities of the United Nations for the maintenance of peace.

2. The States Parties to the present Covenant recognize that, with a view to achieving the full realization of this right:

(a) Primary education shall be compulsory and available free to all;

(b) Secondary education in its different forms, including technical and vocational secondary education, shall be made generally available and accessible to all by every appropriate means, and in particular by the progressive introduction of free education;

(c) Higher education shall be made equally accessible to all, on the basis of capacity, by every appropriate means, and in particular by the progressive introduction of free education;

(d) Fundamental education shall be encouraged or intensified as far as possible for those persons who have not received or completed the whole period of their primary education;

(e) The development of a system of schools at all levels shall be actively pursued, an adequate fellowship system shall be established, and the material conditions of teaching staff shall be continuously improved.

3. The States Parties to the present Covenant *undertake to have respect for the liberty of parents* and, when applicable, legal guardians *to choose for their children schools, other than those established by the public authorities,* which conform to such minimum educational standards as may be laid down or approved by the State and to ensure the religious and moral education of their children in conformity with their own convictions.

4. No part of this article shall be construed so as to interfere with the liberty of individuals and bodies to establish and direct educational institutions, subject always to the observance of the principles set forth in paragraph 1 of this article and to the requirement that the education given in such institutions shall conform to such minimum standards as may be laid down by the State.

International Covenant on Economic,
Social and Cultural Rights (Italics added)

All changes begin by questioning reality. This surfaces the problems, the needs for change, and leads to action. This in turn raises more questions. This dialectical process, ideally, moves us continuously towards our goals.

It was early 1978 in Bolama, a town in the interior of Guinea-Bissau, in West Africa, where I understood in a very simple and beautiful way the meaning of EDUCATION. Delegations of more than fifty educators from the five Portuguese-speaking African countries—Angola, Mozambique, Cape Verde, Sao Tome e Principe, and Guinea-Bissau—together with a group of observers from several European countries and the United States were visiting several educational projects in Bolama.

After seeing two schools, we all gathered in a small stadium where a group of children had staged a play for us. The play was divided in two parts. The first one, characterizing the old colonial school, began with a teacher scolding two children for wearing their African dresses to school and saying, "Haven't you been taught to dress like people?" She questioned them about issues related to their "mother country," Portugal. The children appeared totally ignorant about their own country; in fact, they had no concept of a country of their own. The second part of the play dealt with children in the schools after liberation of Guinea-Bissau. It portrayed children as knowledgeable and proud of their history and their culture, proud of being Africans, proud of their heroes: children who were learning about the realities of their country and the ways they could get involved in them.

These were precisely the themes being discussed by the visiting educators among whom were the Ministers of Education of the five Portuguese-speaking African countries. They met in Bissau from 15-24 February 1978 in the first meeting of Ministers of Education of Angola, Cape Verde, Guinea-Bissau, Mozambique and Sao Tome e Principe. The meeting's objective, according to participants' own words, was "to reflect together on our common educational experiences," and to learn from each other the different methods and approaches to education being developed by each country.

Chiqui Vicioso is from the Dominican Republic. She became familiar with Paulo Freire's methodology while working in New York City with the Dominican immigrant community. Formerly a Seminar Designer with The United Methodist Church's Joint Seminar Program on National and International Affairs, she is currently a graduate student at Columbia Teacher's College, New York City.

Issues Discussed at the Meeting
Historical Role of Education

The first step toward understanding the role that a given educational system plays in a society is to analyze its historical function in that society. In the case of these five countries the analysis was facilitated because they shared a common heritage: Portuguese colonialism. Previous to liberation in 1975-76, their educational systems were conditioned by the particular needs of Portuguese colonialism. The historical functions and features of that educational system were discussed in a workshop entitled "Education and Social Inequality" and were outlined as follows:

Education as a vehicle for colonial ideology: This can be easily understood from the description of the first part of the play we saw in Bolama dealing with the schools during the colonial period. Then "all technical and scientific knowledge that could be transmitted was in the context of a process of assimilation and cultural uprooting" and the function of the colonial education was "to remove the African student from his/her country and to identify him/her with the values and institutions of the colonial metropolis."

Education as an essential element in the maintenance of colonial institutions: Education helped train a local elite of civil servants to operate the administrative apparatus created to enforce colonial policies.

Education as a tool to institutionalize social inequality: During colonial times, education was available only to the members of a local elite from the urban centers. The masses of people, mainly the peasants, were excluded from the educational system—and as a result the division in the population was perpetuated and institutionalized. In Guinea-Bissau, for example, only five percent of the population had access to education during the colonial period. Education became associated with class in the social structure established by the Portuguese colonialists.

Within a colonial context, education as a "right for everyone" runs counter to the principles underlying the socio-economic and political system.

Education During and After the Struggle for National Liberation

Education as a right for all citizens: From the beginning, one of the main goals of the liberation movements was to create the conditions to make education available to all the people. The installation of a school network in the liberated zones took place simultaneously with armed struggle; the school network progressed and expanded simultaneously with the armed struggle. In Guinea-Bissau, for example, the number of students attending school the year before national liberation was 50,593. One year after liberation it jumped to 90,331.

The five nations agreed to take immediate steps to "democratize" their educational systems. Some of these steps included:

1) the creation of an Adult Education Program with the assistance of the Institute of Cultural Action (IDAC) Team directed by Paulo Freire.

2) the acceleration of literacy campaigns.

3) special attention to the educational needs of the rural areas.

Education for the formation of the new person: As stated by the five African nations participating in the meeting, education must seek to develop "free, conscious and cultured men and women, aware of their responsibilities and capable of harmoniously linking personal with collective demands." Education should also aim at integrating the students within their community, inspiring in them a pride in their own culture, promoting critical, disciplined and responsible attitudes towards social justice and universal culture.

This statement of purposes led to the following resolves:

• to link, at the national level, the educational system with the planning of the country's socio-economic development.

• to relate theory and practice through an inter-disciplinary methodology, and to progressively introduce productive work as part of the school's curriculum.

• to connect the role played by the school to the needs of the community in which it is located.

• to promote the African cultural values by developing the national languages.

Each of these aims was discussed in depth by the participant delegations in four workshops established for that purpose during the meeting. The workshops were entitled: Education and Social Inequality; Education and Economic Development; Education and Cultural Identity; Education and Knowledge.

By engaging in the process briefly described above, the Portuguese-speaking nations of Africa are setting an example by openly questioning their past and acting on it, and by continuing to question their present with the aim of creating a better future. Education is a fundamental tool for the formation of a critical mind capable of engaging in this process. This is why the struggle to make education a Human Right is essential for the progress of humanity.

The problems and solutions proposed and discussed by the five sponsoring nations transcended geographi-cal boundaries and may shed some light on the problems facing educational systems in the West. A useful lesson drawn from the meeting was the relevance of historical analysis.

In analyzing the historical role of education in their own societies, the five African nations related the needs of the colonial system to the role assumed by their educational system. This kind of analysis is rarely done. The gap between the theory of education and its *actual function* in society is not always recognized.

In most highly industrialized countries, "access" to education is an established principle, at least at the elementary and secondary levels. This principle has led to the widely accepted notion that education in these countries is free and available to everybody. However, the subjective acceptance of this principle frequently prevents a critical evaluation of the educational system's reality. Such an evaluation should include the following questions:

1. Is education really available to all in our society?

2. What are the qualitative differences in the education received by different classes and racial groups in our society?

3. How is education financed in our country?

4. What are the chances of everyone going beyond certain educational levels in our country?

5. Does the educational system perpetuate discrimination based on race, sex, language, religion and political or other opinion? Describe how.

6. Is there a selection process in the educational system? How does it work? Who benefits?

These questions all address themselves to the heart of the issue—the value structure reflected in our educational system:

1. What are these values?

2. What are the values of our society?

3. Are the values of our society strengthened or weakened by the educational system?

Exercises for Reflection

1. Relate this chapter to Article 13 of the International Covenant on Economic, Social and Cultural Rights (at the beginning of this chapter).

   a. What does Article 13 say? Should it go further? Would you add or change anything? What about education for persons with a disability? What about an educational system which must take into account a society with different languages and cultural backgrounds? Other differences?

   b. How do you react to the content of the

chapter in relationship to Article 13? Radical change was necessary in Guinea-Bissau, Mozambique, Angola, Cape Verde, Sao Tome e Principe, for a just educational system to have a chance. What changes might be necessary for our society to offer a better educational system? Would this necessitate political action? Should the Church participate? Recall Dwain Epps' introduction to Section II: "...A measure of equality in employment or education is granted. But it cannot be assumed that by multiplying the amelioration of individual symptoms a basic social ill is cured...." Would this be true in our society? What would we need to do to change?

2. Discuss Jesus' way of teaching. What were his methods? What were the values he imparted to his people? What did he wish his people to do...to be? What does this say to us today?

Resources

Looking at Guinea-Bissau: A New Nation's Development Strategy by Denis Goulet. "...Education is assigned a comprehensive role in Guinea-Bissau's development strategy. One-fifth of the country's public budget goes to education; the Ministry of Education accounts for the greatest volume of public expenditure." Published by Overseas Development Council, 1717 Massachusetts Avenue, N.W., Washington, D.C. 20036. $2.50.

Some of the inspiration for the educational system in Guinea-Bissau comes from the philosophy and methodology of the exiled Brazilian educator Paulo Freire, a staff member of the World Council of Churches. Several of his books have already challenged people in both the United States and Canada:

1. *Pedagogy of the Oppressed* (New York: Herder and Herder, 1970).

2. *Cultural Action for Freedom* (Cambridge: Center for the Study of Development and Social Change and Harvard Educational Review, 1970).

3. *Education for Critical Consciousness* (New York: Seabury Press, Inc., 1973).

4. *Pedagogy in Process: Letters to Guinea-Bissau* (New York: Seabury Press, Inc., 1978).

The Institute for Cultural Action (IDAC) was created by Paulo Freire and works with the Ministry of Education of Guinea-Bissau on its literacy campaign. IDAC was also present during the conference in 1978 with the educators and Ministers of Education of the five Portuguese-speaking African countries. IDAC came into being in 1971 and in its own words described itself as "an international and interdisciplin-

ary team which, working in close collaboration with Professor Paulo Freire (chairman of IDAC Executive Committee), has as its main area of interest the theory and practice of *conscientisation* as a liberating instrument in the processes of education, development and social change."

IDAC sees conscientisation as "the process through which men and women become aware of their socio-cultural reality, overcome the alienations and constraints to which they are subjected and affirm themselves as conscious, creative subjects of their own history."[1]

IDAC has a publication which is issued periodically. Their address is 27 Chemin des Crets, 1218 Grand Saconnex, Geneva, Switzerland. No. 11/12 (Winter 1975, Spring 1976) was entitled *Guinea-Bissau, Re-Inventing Education.* No. 14 was entitled *Reconstructing Social Awareness: A Socio-Pedagogical Experience in Industrial Society.* 4 issues will be sent for $8, or $12 (air mail outside Europe).

Adult Illiteracy in the United States: A Report to the Ford Foundation by Carmen St. John Hunter and David Harman (New York: McGraw Hill, to be published in spring 1979).

Liberation as an Aim of the Church's Educational Work, by Else M. Adjali and Carolyn McIntyre. This monograph (#12) might be helpful to Christians as they seek to understand and participate in the liberation struggle, in the struggles for human rights. Board of Discipleship of the United Methodist Church. Order from Discipleship Resources, P. O. Box 840, Nashville, TN 37202. $1.95.

"A Minor Altercation"—A dramatized account of an inter-racial incident in a Boston public school. After getting into a fight, two high school girls—one Black, one white—are sent home, and their families are forced to become involved in settling the dispute. Dramatically presents approaches to racial tension. 30 minutes. Available from Tricontinental Film Center, 333 Avenue of the Americas, New York, N.Y. 10014.

"Bullets Are Beginning To Flower"—This fascinating Dutch film looks at the transformation of the Mozambican school system since independence. In so doing, it provides a unique glimpse at how the new government is actually implementing its vision of building a new society. 27 minutes. Produced by IKON-Kenmerk (Holland), 1977: Rental $40. Available from Southern Africa Media Center, 630 Natoma Street, San Francisco, California 94103.

---

1. *Institute for Cultural Action*—a descriptive pamphlet, 1973.

CHAPTER 11
TO TRANSFORM SYSTEMS DEALING WITH CONFLICTS AND CRIMES
FAY HONEY KNOPP

Article 9

1. Everyone has the *right to liberty and security of person.* No one shall be subjected to *arbitrary arrest or detention.* No one shall be deprived of his (her) liberty except on such grounds and in accordance with such procedures as are established by law.

2. Anyone who is *arrested* shall be *informed,* at the time of arrest, of the *reasons for his (her) arrest* and shall be promptly *informed of any charges* against him (her).

3. Anyone arrested or detained on a criminal charge shall be brought *promptly before a judge* or other officer authorized by law to exercise judicial power and shall be *entitled to trial within a reasonable time* or to release. It shall not be the general rule that persons awaiting trial shall be detained in custody, but release may be subject to guarantees to appear for trial, at any other stage of the judicial proceedings, and, should occasion arise, for execution of the judgement.

4. Anyone who is deprived of his (her) liberty by arrest or detention shall be entitled to take proceedings before a court, in order that that court may decide without delay on the lawfulness of his (her) detention and order his (her) release if the detention is not lawful.

5. Anyone who has been the victim of unlawful arrest or detention shall have an enforceable right to compensation.

Article 10

1. All persons deprived of their liberty shall be *treated with humanity and with respect for the inherent dignity of the human person.*

2. (*a*) Accused persons shall, save in exceptional circumstances, be segregated from convicted persons and shall be subject to separate treatment appropriate to their status as unconvicted persons;

(*b*) Accused juvenile persons shall be separated from adults and brought as speedily as possible for adjudication.

3. The penitentiary system shall comprise treatment of prisoners the essential aim of which shall be their *reformation and social rehabilitation.* Juvenile offenders shall be segregated from adults and be accorded treatment appropriate to their age and legal status.

Article 11

No one shall be imprisoned merely on the ground of inability to fulfill a contractual obligation.

Article 14

1. *All persons shall be equal before the courts* and tribunals. In the determination of any criminal charge against him (her), or of his (her) rights and obligations in a suit at law, everyone shall be *entitled to a fair and public hearing* by a *competent, independent and impartial tribunal* established by law. The Press and the public may be excluded from all or part of a trial for reasons of morals, public order or national security in a democratic society, or when the interest of the private lives of the parties so requires, or to the extent strictly necessary in the opinion of the court in special circumstances where publicity would prejudice the interests of justice; but any judgement rendered in a criminal case or in a suit at law shall be made public except where the interest of juvenile persons otherwise requires or the proceedings concern matrimonial disputes or the guardianship of children.

2. Everyone charged with a criminal offence shall have the *right to be presumed innocent until proved guilty* according to law.

3. In the determination of any criminal charge against him (her) everyone shall be entitled to the following minimum guarantees, in full equality:

(a) *To be informed promptly* and in detail in a language which he (she) understands of the *nature and cause of the charge* against him (her);

(b) To have adequate *time and facilities for the preparation* of his (her) defence and to communicate with counsel of his (her) own choosing;

(c) To be *tried without undue delay;*

(d) To be *tried in his (her) presence, and to defend him(her)self* in person or through legal assistance of his (her) own choosing; to be informed, if he (she) does not have legal assistance, of this right; and *to have legal assistance assigned to him (her),* in any case where the interests of justice so require, and without payment by him (her) in any such case if he (she) does not have sufficient means to pay for it;

(e) *To examine, or have examined, the witnesses* against him (her) and to obtain the attendance and examination of witnesses on his (her) behalf under the same conditions as witnesses against him (her);

(f) To have the *free assistance of an interpreter* if he (she) cannot understand or speak the language used in court;

(g) *Not be compelled to testify against him(her)self or to confess guilt.*

4. In the case of juvenile persons, the procedure shall be such as will take account of their age and the desirability of promoting their rehabilitation.

5. Everyone convicted of a crime shall have *the right to his (her) conviction and sentence being reviewed* by a higher tribunal according to law.

6. When a person has by a final decision been convicted of a criminal offence and when subsequently his (her) conviction has been reversed or he (she) has been pardoned on the ground that a new or newly discovered fact shows conclusively that there has been a *miscarriage of justice, the person* who has suffered punishment as a result of such conviction shall be *compensated according to law,*

unless it is proved that the non-disclosure of the unknown fact in time is wholly or partly attributable to him (her).

7. *No one shall be liable to be tried or punished again for an offence for which he (she) has already been finally convicted or acquitted* in accordance with the law and penal procedure of each country.

Article 15

1. *No one shall be held guilty of any criminal offence on account of any act or omission which did not constitute a criminal offence, under national or international law, at the time when it was committed.* Nor shall a heavier penalty be imposed than the one that was applicable at the time when the criminal offence was committed. If, subsequent to the commission of the offence, provision is made by law for the imposition of a lighter penalty, the offender shall benefit thereby.

2. Nothing in this article shall prejudice the trial and punishment of any person for any act or omission which, at the time when it was committed, was criminal according to the general principles of law recognized by the community of nations.

Article 16

Everyone shall have the right to recognition everywhere as a person before the law.

International Covenant on Civil and Political Rights (Italics added)

I've been engaged in a special alternative ministry to federal prisoners for the last 22 years. As a result of these experiences, I speak from an emotional as well as a research perspective. I inherited a system of injustice I did not create. My goal is action: to transform present systems that deal with conflicts and crimes into more just processes.

It is difficult to address prison injustice briefly in the vacuum created by the lack of a coherent prison-change movement. Occasionally prisoners flash their desperate message by erupting in an Attica or a Tombs uprising. But generally the issues surrounding these lawless, violent institutions are not well-defined. Concepts of crime and justice are shaped primarily by the media, by office-seekers exploiting people's fears, and by the well-funded law enforcement apparatus. The view we are given is a "war" model, with

Fay Honey Knopp, member of the Religious Society of Friends (Quakers), wife, mother, grandmother and activist, is the founder and coordinator of the Prison Research Education Action Project (PREAP) in Westport, Connecticut.

suggested solutions of more punishments, more weapons, more prisons. We hear about "justice" from the powerful—those who carry it out. Where are the voices that can speak about "justice" from the perspectives of the receivers of the system?

The Prison Research Education Action Project (PREAP) was conceived to develop some new concepts for a just system. *Instead of Prisons, A Handbook for Abolitionists* is our first tool for use by the movement we hope to build. We have developed structured workshop methods to raise consciousness about the realities of crime and justice, and to prepare trained facilitators to carry these new and challenging ideas into action.

In the workshops participants begin by brainstorming a list of conditions that encourage crimes, together with a corresponding list of responses to reduce crimes. Lists of some ways crime can be reduced usually include full employment; an end to racism; equal access for all to wealth and power; a decent standard of living; good housing; the abolition of handguns; better education; a culture that encourages non-violence; and conciliation opportunities for criminals to make restitution to victims. Workshop participants quickly discover for themselves new long-range goals: instead of cages, the creation of caring community—a social kingdom in which justice means the equal availability to all of liberty, opportunity, income, and a basis of self-respect. Though genuine solutions to criminal conditions in no way relate to the imprisonment or execution of wrongdoers, our society, I fear, is headed down this repressive road unless *we* put on the brakes. *We* are the resources for change.

In the workshops we try to rid ourselves of myths about prisons. We expose the myth that prisons deter crime or protect the public in any real way, when they in fact create crime. In the words of former Attorney General Edward Levi: "It does not seem to appear that persons who have spent time in prison are less likely to commit crime again. Perhaps indeed they are more likely to do so, because prisons are learning places for crime".

We expose the myth that prisons rehabilitate. In fact, their primary function is control and punishment of a particular segment of society. For the nine million crimes reported annually, only 1.5 percent of the perpetrators end up in prison and they come basically from the minorities, the youth, and the poor.

We expose the myth that punishment by prison "works." The public seems willing to accept the fact that punishment is no solution in at least one large category of crime: family crime. Instead of sending abusive parents to prison, we are beginning to learn that re-educating them in the skills of parenting and child-nurturing, and helping them reduce unbearable stress from their environment, are better responses. (See Chapter 9, "To Promote the General Welfare.") Our workshops extend these alternative responses to almost all kinds of criminal situations.

We expose the myth that prisons are worth the cost. They are, in fact, the most expensive method of punishment ever devised. Prisons in the United States are a billion-dollar industry, larger than many giant corporations. Bolstered by powerful lobbies, plans for building approximately 1,000 additional prisons and jails are now in the works. It costs from $30,000 to $50,000 to construct an individual cage. It costs from $10,000 to $26,000 to keep one person behind bars for a year. In New York City the two-year imprisonment of a person found guilty of a $200 burglary can cost the taxpayer an average of $52,000, plus court and parole costs. Among many additional hidden costs is the fact that prisoners' families usually go on welfare. There is no way to measure the human costs. For instance, 80 percent of the imprisoned women are mothers; 38 percent of these lose custody of their children.

Ultimately it is not an economic question but a moral one. You may believe that slavery has been abolished in the United States. This is not so. The Thirteenth Amendment in our Constitution which abolished *plantation* slavery also states that if an individual has been convicted of a crime it is *legal* to enslave him/her: "Neither slavery nor involuntary servitude, *except* as a punishment for crime whereof the party shall have been duly convicted, shall exist within the United States, or any place subject to their jurisdiction."*

Prisoners are the "exceptions." They are held in dehumanizing circumstances just as plantation slaves once were. Besides all other deprivations and prison punishments, prisoners are not paid for their labor or are paid very little; they are denied work-persons' compensation, the right to organize, the right to vote, and most other constitutional rights guaranteed every American citizen. So long as a prison system is in existence, we—you and I—are slave holders. We must continue the movement started by slave abolitionists of the past, until *all* slavery is abolished.

"Abolition" is a process. The abolishing process seeks to *gradually* and continually limit and diminish the function of prisons. In our workshops we formulate an "attrition model" to help us define this process. Although I won't name all the alternatives here, I will say that in this society we've always had them. But it's the well-to-do who have access to alternatives, and mainly the poor and the powerless who get stuck in prisons. We've *always* had schools for "exceptional youth who are unreachable by means of conventional educational methods"—i.e., schools for juvenile delinquents, if you are poor. We've always had psychiatric services, drying-out hospitals, drugs prescribed by physicians, counseling programs, sex re-education programs, mediation services, vocational aptitude tests. It is primarily the black, tan, poor and powerless folks who don't have access to these services and alternatives. These possibilities must be made universally available.

In principle, we advocate minimum intervention in the life of the wrongdoer and maximum protection to the public. In practice this translates into programs

*Also see Article 8 of the Covenant on Civil and Political Rights preceding Chapter 2.

that provide care and empowerment for all victims, and the least damaging sanction for the offender.

In almost all criminal situations there's some sanction other than imprisonment that can properly respond to behavior. In Albuquerque, New Mexico, for instance, a community storefront provides services for sex offenders. These services should be available in every community.

Rape, like most behavior, is learned. A model for reducing crimes of rape is described in detail in *Instead of Prisons.* It includes: (1) a re-education process for the rapist and the public; (2) caring for and empowering victims to resist and prevent victimization. This is a liberation model, not a war model. Prisons do not lessen victims' pain, re-educate rapists, or genuinely protect society. Secure and humane settings outside prison walls are already successfully serving violent sex offenders. But there are too few such programs.

Prisons are a billion-dollar failure. They are a social problem in themselves. They create new, serious social problems. We need to say that loudly and often. We must learn how to strategize and design alternatives to cages in our society. While there will never be a complete blueprint, there are many tested responses to conflicts and crimes that contribute to a safer, more just society.

We must build a movement with the capacity to take the first step in social change—which is to see the need for the new. In the second stage, the creative one, we must create the vehicles to bring new ideas into the community and translate them into programs and services for all people. We believe we have begun the first stage and are strategizing for the second stage. We need the help of the religious community if we are to succeed.

I am a Quaker. I do not, in my living, separate religion and politics. I am a political person because I am led to be; led to challenge and speak truth to the centers of power. We must empower ourselves to change the unjust. We are called upon to act.

We must move toward a system that seeks to restore both the wronged and wrongdoer to lives of integrity in our communities: a system that speaks to the Christian belief in loving kindness toward every neighbor, speaks to the golden rule of universal benevolence, the Moslem principle of oneness in community. We must move toward a system that speaks to the Jewish principle of steadfast love binding the community, and to the Quaker principle of the Christ within all human beings, including the caged.

As long as one person remains in prison, Jesus remains in prison. Jesus had nothing to say to unjust systems except to deny their power over him. He said in effect: "Violence stops here, caging stops here." Let this be our testimony to the whole world.

Questions for Reflection

1. Relate the content of this chapter to Articles 10, 11, 14, 15, 16 of the Covenant on Civil and Political Rights (at the beginning of this chapter). Would an "abolitionist" rewrite Article 10 or any of the other Articles of the Covenant?

2. Honey Knopp feels that when we hear about "justice" we hear it from the "powerful...those who carry it out" but "where are the voices that can speak about 'justice' from the perspectives of the receivers of the system?" Relate these statements to Dwain Epps' introduction of this Section: "Human relations are largely governed by the distribution of power in society...." How do you feel about these statements? What are the implications for Christians seeking to love?

3. Honey Knopp feels that she cannot separate religion and politics. She feels that she must be about transforming present systems that deal with conflicts and crimes, moving instead to a more just process. Do you feel that that is the role for a Christian? Is that what is meant by Jesus when he said, "...when in prison you visited me..."? Read Matthew 25:31-46.

Exercises for Reflection

1. The best way to get involved in the crucial issues of Criminal Justice is:

(a) to learn more about the Prison Research Education Action Project titled *Instead of Prisons: A Handbook for Abolitionists,* Prison Research Education Action Project, 3049 East Genesee St., Syracuse, New York 13224. ($6.50 plus .50¢ postage and handling.)

(b) to participate in a workshop as developed by the Project: *Workshop Manual: Instead of Prisons.* Order from Prison Research Education Action Project, address same as above. (1-9 copies, $2.00 per copy plus .35¢ postage; 10 or more copies, $1.75 per copy plus postage.)

2. In 1980 the Sixth United Nations Congress on the Prevention of Crime and the Treatment of Offenders will be held. Find out from your government representatives how the United States/Canada will participate in such a conference. Who gets a chance to *inform* the representatives participating in such a

meeting? Through what channels or organizations can citizens be part of the debate which the international community holds periodically? How are the debates from such conferences made public?

3. Throughout the world there are thousands of people who end up in prisons because of their political or religious beliefs and actions. "While torture is sometimes applied to common prisoners, the victims are most likely persons who have become involved in the struggle for injustice and human rights in their own societies, people who have had the courage to voice the needs of the people. In the face of political opposition, rulers of an increasing number of countries have decreed emergency laws in which the basic guarantee of habeas corpus is suspended. Detainees are forbidden contact with a defense lawyer, their families, religious leaders, or others, creating conditions propitious for torture. Under the pretext of 'national security,' many states today subordinate human dignity to the selfish interests of those in power." (See the WCC Statement, Chapter 3.) Are there political prisoners in the United States or Canada?

Preparing for Effective Witness: Further Reading
"The Most Discriminatory Sentence," Chapter 10.
"Torture," Chapter 3.

Resources
"The Jail" —A documentary filmed in San Francisco, showing the constraints of a county jail system through interviews with prisoners and their jailers. Their personalities and frustrations are exposed, as is the lifestyle in an American prison. 81 minutes. Black & white. Available from Cinema 5, 595 Madison Avenue, New York, N.Y. 10022. Rental $85 if no admission charged; $150 if admission.

"Wilmington 10, Wilmington 1000"—Feature-length documentary which focuses on political prisoners in the U.S. The film uses a family/community perspective to clarify the sociological implications of political imprisonment and human rights. It centers on the Wilmington 10 case: nine Black men and one white woman jailed in North Carolina for purportedly setting fire to a grocery store. Available from Haile Gerima, School of Communications, Howard University, Washington, D.C. 20059.

"Voices From Within" —Interviews with long-term women prisoners in the Bedford Hills prison, New York. Helps one to see the effects of incarceration on the individual. 20 minutes. Available from Pacific Street Films, 280 Clinton Street, Brooklyn, New York 11201.

REFLECTIONS ON SECTION II

THE STRUGGLE FOR THE DEFENSE AND PROMOTION OF HUMAN RIGHTS INVOLVES RECOURSE TO POLITICAL ACTION

Agreeing to Be Part of the Struggles

The Preamble of the two Human Rights Covenants is clear that "...the ideal of free human beings enjoying civil and political freedom and freedom from fear and want can only be achieved if conditions are created whereby everyone may enjoy his (her) civil and political rights, as well as his (her) economic, social and cultural rights...." Do those conditions exist? If not, who should create them? What are the obstacles? Is anyone struggling to create those conditions? Is the struggle political? Should Christians be involved?

Quickly review each of the chapters in Section II, looking for the political action or goals suggested as necessary to defend or promote the human rights in question in each chapter. Consider also whether these actions will "change the structures of society in the direction of greater justice and equality." (See introduction of Section II.) Use the spaces following each chapter title shown below to list:

1. Your agreements or disagreements with the actions taken by Christians as described.
2. Alternatives to political action by Christians. (Explain.)

Chapter 7: "To Restore the Economic Health of the Community" (Articles 6 & 7 of the International Covenant on Economic, Social and Cultural Rights)

Chapter 8: "To Secure a Correction of Abuses" (Article 8 of the International Covenant on Economic, Social and Cultural Rights)

Chapter 9: "To Promote the General Welfare" (Article 23 of the International Covenant on Civil and Political Rights)

Chapter 10: "To Democratize the System of Education" (Article 13 of the International Covenant on Economic, Social and Cultural Rights)

Chapter 11: "To Transform Systems Dealing With Conflict and Crimes" (Articles 9, 10, 11, 14, 15, 16 of the International Covenant on Civil and Political Rights)

Check the chapters in Section I. What are Christians doing about self-determination, about apartheid, about aliens, about involvement in public affairs and about racism? Are these actions part of the human rights struggles? Are you personally involved in any of these struggles? Do you feel you should be? In your own words describe how your faith helps you understand the need to be involved in the human rights struggles.

What do these passages in the New Testament mean for us today? Luke 4:18; Matthew 25:40; Luke 6:46-49; Matthew 23:23; Ephesians 6:12; Colossians 2:15; James 5:4-5; John 10:10; James 2:20-26. (There are many more we might ponder.)

The Rev. Robert Smith of the Scarboro Foreign Mission Society in Canada gives us his statement of faith:

Our faith calls us to a participation in God's work in the world. We Canadians find ourselves assaulted in these years by doubts, fears and especially by guilt. It is very easy to trigger in our conscience as Christians a negative response. Since there is nothing very Christian in doubts, fears, and guilt, not much is going to happen as a result of that kind of negative energy. We are to use another energy, the conviction of God being with us now, re-creating our world in the midst of those who struggle for justice and human dignity. We can offer our world a Christian dynamic: a living, positive, joyful and hope-filled participation in God's presence. "Now God's home is with men and women! He will live with them and they shall be His people. God Himself will be with them, and He will be their God. He will wipe away all tears from their eyes. There will be no more death, no more grief, crying, or pain. The old things have disappeared." [1] (Rev. 21:3-4)

Do we believe in the promise of "a new heaven and a new earth"? (Isaiah 65:17-25 and Revelation 21:1-4) How do we express that belief here and now? Rosemary Radford Ruether is convinced that Christians are awaiting "a new burst of that God-given energy and grace" which will enable them "to tackle the great questions of our day: economic injustice, lingering racism, sexism, rampant militarism and patterns of consumerism that pollute the earth and threaten the very foundations of human life on earth. In the words of Moses in Deuteronomy... 'I have set before you this day life and death, blessing and curse; therefore choose life, that you and your descendants may live.'" [2]

However, I'm not sure we are waiting. I believe that Christians are acting throughout the world. Examples in this study book are a good testimony. Robert Smith, in his article in *Mission Magazine,* suggests some questions which may help Christians to reflect on their own feelings regarding political action.

1. In what ways can we say that we have had an experience of God's presence in our lives or in the world around us?

---

1. "Believing Is Seeing" by Robert Smith, pp. 21-23 in *Mission Magazine,* June 1978, United Church of Canada.
2. Wolfgang Roth and Rosemary Radford Ruether, *The Liberating Bond,* p. 83.

2. Do you think that Canadian (and U.S.) Christians respond to the problems of the world in a moralistic way or rather as a joyful participation in God's action in the world?

3. How do you think the Church ought to relate to the power that is represented in our economic institutions?

4. What do you think is the strength that is proper to the Christian Church? For example, to use its political clout to use moral persuasion, to pray, to denounce in a prophetic manner or to slowly awaken the consciousness of its members?

5. Do you think that the leadership of the Church is sufficiently communicating its concerns and activities to the membership of the Church?[3]

In agreeing to be part of the struggles, you may wish to test yourself and write your own chapter on the rights which have not been dealt with in this study book. They are included in Article 15 of the International Covenant on Economic, Social and Cultural Rights:

1. The States Parties to the present Covenant recognize the right of everyone:

(a) To take part in cultural life;

(b) To enjoy the benefits of scientific progress and its applications;

(c) To benefit from the protection of the moral and material interests resulting from any scientific, literary or artistic production of which he (she) is the author.

2. The steps to be taken by the States Parties to the present Covenant to achieve the full realization of this right shall include those necessary for the conservation, the development and the diffusion of science and culture.

3. The States Parties to the present Covenant undertake to respect the freedom indispensable for scientific research and creative activity.

4. The States Parties to the present Covenant recognize the benefits to be derived from the encouragement and development of international contacts and co-operation in the scientific and cultural fields.

This chapter should include an understanding of the implications of the rights described in Article 15: the moral and ethical issues raised by these rights. Perhaps some specific cases could be described to illustrate the promotion or the violation of these rights in the United States or Canada or in any other country. Your chapter should also include some questions or exercises as well as resources and organizations which could be useful. Finally, your chapter should suggest those actions necessary to guarantee these rights and a decision about your personal involvement in defending these rights.

In writing this chapter, take into consideration the statement by Dwain Epps in the introduction to Section II. It is probable that the "racially, economically and politically oppressed of the world" are the ones who do not have the right to participate in cultural life, the right to enjoy the benefits of scientific progress or the right to benefit from the protection of the moral and material interests resulting from any scientific, literary or artistic production of which they are the authors. How would you redress this "imbalance of power"? What would be the task of the church in helping to guarantee these rights for all people?

---

3. Smith, p. 23.

SECTION III

UNIVERSAL HUMAN RIGHTS APPLY TO OUR OWN SITUATION AS WELL AS TO OTHERS

INTRODUCTION

Few nations openly oppose the ideals of human rights, yet over the past two decades much more attention has been given to the splinter in the eye of the other than to the log in one's own....

Only when nations, peoples, and churches begin to wrestle with their own problems can progress be made, and only when we strive to support our brothers and sisters in other lands in their similar efforts to achieve greater justice in their own socio-economic, cultural, and political contexts will we be able to say that our commitment to the well-being of all men and women is greater than our will to impose our own patterns on them for better or for worse.

Dwain Epps

CHAPTER 12
TO ENSURE AVAILABILITY OF FOOD FOR ALL
MIA ADJALI

Article 11

1. The States Parties to the present Covenant recognize the right of everyone *to an adequate standard of living for himself (herself) and his (her) family,* including adequate *food, clothing and housing,* and to the continuous improvement of living conditions. The States Parties will take appropriate steps to ensure the realization of this right, recognizing to this effect the essential importance of international co-operation based on free consent.

2. The States Parties to the present Covenant, recognizing the fundamental right of everyone *to be free from hunger,* shall take, individually and through international co-operation, the measures, including specific programmes, which are needed:

(a) To improve methods of production, conservation and distribution of food by making full use of technical and scientific knowledge, by disseminating knowledge of the principles of nutrition and by developing or reforming agrarian systems in such a way as to achieve the most efficient development and utilization of natural resources;

(b) Taking into account the problems of both food-importing and food-exporting countries, to ensure an equitable distribution of world food supplies in relation to need.

International Covenant on Economic,
Social and Cultural Rights (Italics added)

In 1975 the Institute for Food and Development Policy was created, firmly believing that by "identifying the underlying social causes of hunger, food issues become vehicles for profound social change." Two members of the Institute, Frances Moore Lappe and Joseph Collins, wrote a book in 1977 titled *Food First: Beyond the Myth of Scarcity.* This is a useful book which can be a vehicle for those interested in deepening or challenging their own involvement in these issues. The central themes of their book have been expressed in a short essay entitled, *World Hunger, Ten Myths.*[1]

In countering the myths, the authors list Ten Food Self-Reliance Fundamentals which, they suggest, "could ground a coherent and vital movement."

1. Every country in the world has the resources

necessary for its people to free themselves from hunger.

2. To balance the planet's population and resources, we must now address the root cause of both hunger and high birth rates: the insecurity and poverty of the majority that results from the control over basic national resources by a few.

3. Hunger is only made worse when approached as a technical problem. Hunger can only be overcome by the transformation of social relationships in which the majority directly participate in building a democratic economic system.

4. Political and economic inequalities are the greatest stumbling block to development.

5. Safeguarding the world's agricultural environment and people freeing themselves from hunger are complementary goals.

6. Agriculture must become, first and foremost, a way for people to produce the food they need and secondarily a possible source of foreign exchange.

7. Our food security is not threatened by hungry

---

1. Francis Moore Lappe and Joseph Collins, *World Hunger, Ten Myths* (San Francisco: Institute for Food and Development Policy, 1977, revised 1978).

people but by a system that concentrates economic power into the hands of elites who profit by the generation of scarcity and the internationalization of food control.

8. Today, in every country in the world, people are working to democratize the control over food-producing resources.

9. Escape from hunger comes not through the redistribution of food, but only through the redistribution of control over food-producing resources.

10. For Americans distressed about the reality of hunger in a world of plenty, the tasks ahead are clear: work to remove those obstacles preventing people from taking charge of their food-producing resources —obstacles that today are being built by our government, by U.S.-supported international agencies and U.S.-based corporations. Our work toward food self-reliance and democratization of our own economy allies us with the struggle of people in underdeveloped countries fighting for food self-determination.

The final statement defines clearly the way we can "help" the world to be free from hunger. Our responsibilities are at home. In their book the authors conclude that "people will feed themselves." While keeping in mind the "fundamentals" cited above, they suggest that "the real obstacle in the way of people feeding themselves is that the majority of citizens in every market economy are increasingly cut out from control over productive resources." Thus the real lessons for us are these:

First: We cannot solve the problem of world hunger for other people. They must do that for themselves. We can, however, work to remove the obstacles that make it increasingly difficult for people everywhere to take control of food production and feed themselves.

Second: We should focus on removing those obstacles that are being reinforced today by forces originating in our country, often in our name and with our tax money.

Third: We must support people everywhere already resisting forced food dependency and now building new self-reliant societies in which the majority of people directly control food-producing resources. Direct financial assistance is important, as is communicating their very existence to Americans still believing that "people are too oppressed ever to change."

Fourth: Working for self-reliance, both on a personal and national level, benefits everyone. Making America less dependent on importing its food and less dependent on pushing our food on others will be a step toward making America "safe for the world." Local self-reliance will make it more difficult for elites, both in the industrial countries and the underdeveloped countries, to manipulate prices, wages, and people for their own profit. Self-reliance for America means wholesome food available to all, supplied by a healthy domestic agriculture of widely dispersed control.

For the readers of this study whose interest may have been stimulated by these points, the first responsibility is to research the content. The following questions may help prompt some reactions.

1. What is your initial reaction to each statement?

2. What from your own experience would make you agree or disagree with each statement?

3. How could you best research these statements beyond reading the book *Food First* or the pamphlet *World Hunger, Ten Myths* which Ms. Moore Lappe and Mr. Collins wrote?

4. How could the "Ten Food Self-Reliance Fundamentals" ground a coherent and vital movement as the authors suggest?

5. What are your fundamental beliefs about "World Hunger"? Are they similar to Moore Lappe's and Collins' or do you feel that it is unfounded to suggest that the following ideas are myths? (Explain.) These are the ten myths which the authors wish to dispel. Note your reactions to each one in the space provided.

Myth One: People are hungry because of scarcity— both of food and land.

Myth Two: There are just too many people for agricultural resources to sustain.

Myth Three: Hunger will be overcome by concentrating on producing more food.

Myth Four: To achieve food security our hungry world must rely on large landholders.

Myth Five: We are faced with a tragic trade-off. A needed increase in food production can come only at the expense of the ecological integrity of our food-producing resources. The use of pesticides will have to be increased even if the risks are great. Farming must be pushed onto marginal lands at the risk of irreparable erosion.

Myth Six: An underdeveloped country's best hope for development is to export crops in which it has a "natural advantage." It can then use the earnings to import food and industrial goods.

Myth Seven: Hunger is a contest between the Rich world and Poor world.

Myth Eight: Peasants are so oppressed, malnourished and conditioned into a state of dependency that they are beyond the point of being able to mobilize themselves.

Myth Nine: Hunger can be solved by redistributing food.

Myth Ten: To solve the problem of hunger we must increase our foreign aid.

Exercise for Reflection

Relate Article 11 of the Covenant on Economic, Social and Cultural Rights (at the beginning of this chapter) to the search for new food systems as suggested in this chapter:

a. To what extent do you feel that the government should be responsible for guaranteeing food, clothing and housing?

b. Examine your own knowledge of production and distribution of food in North America. How can you, as a consumer, participate in the decisions affecting such a vital area in our food system?

Resources

World Hunger: Causes and Remedies by the Staff of the Transnational Institute. A discussion of the world food situation assessing the present crisis, offering background analyses and considering the future outlook. Sixteen tables of comparative past, present, and projected data are included in this article based upon a report prepared for the United Nations World Food Conference in Rome, November 1974. Available from Transnational Institute, 1901 Q Street, N.W., Washington, D.C. 20009.

Food First: Beyond the Myth of Scarcity by Frances Moore Lappe and Joseph Collins with Cary Fowler (Houghton Mifflin, 1977). Available from Institute for Food and Development Policy, 2588 Mission Street, San Francisco, California 94110.

World Hunger: Ten Myths (Revised Edition) by Frances Moore Lappe and Joseph Collins, 1977, revised 1978. Also available from Institute for Food and Development Policy. 1-9 copies, $1.50 each; 10-49 copies, $1.00 each; over 50 copies, 90¢ each.

Food/Hunger Macro-Analysis Seminar: A Do It Yourself Manual by William Moyer and Erika Thorne. Study Action Guide for college courses and action groups. Details organizing technique and curriculum for a participatory seminar examining the structural roots of hunger. $2.50 each or $2.00 for orders of 10 or more. Available from Transnational Academic Program, Institute for World Order, 1140 Avenue of the Americas, New York, N.Y. 10036.

Ideas and Action, Action for Development, FAO, 00100 Rome, Italy.

CERES, FAO Review on Development, UNIPUB, 650 First Avenue, P.O. Box 433, Murray Hill Station, New York, N.Y. 10016.

New Internationalist, published in England, but subscribe through the New World Coalition, Room 209, 409 Boylston Street, Boston, MA 02116.

For information on books and films on Food & Land write: EARTHWORK, 1499 Potrero Avenue, San Francisco, California 94110.

Organizations

INSTITUTE FOR FOOD AND DEVELOPMENT POLICY, 2588 Mission Street, San Francisco, California 94110. Several religious organizations help to support the Institute including the United Presbyterians and the Church of the Brethren. A new magazine, *The Food Monitor,* jointly sponsored with World Hunger Year in New York, is available.

THE TRANSNATIONAL INSTITUTE, 1901 Q Street, N.W., Washington, D.C. 20009, is the international program of the Institute for Policy Studies in Washington. Established in 1973, it centers in London and Amsterdam and addresses fundamental disparity between the rich and poor peoples and nations of the world, investigates its causes, and develops alternatives for its remedy.

TEN DAYS FOR WORLD DEVELOPMENT is a joint development education program of the Anglican, Catholic, Lutheran, Presbyterian and United Churches of Canada. Its goal is to bring about changes in Canadian public policy which will broaden the opportunities for human growth, especially by the peoples of developing countries. For further information contact: Robert Gardner, National Coordinator, Inter-Church Committee for World Development Education, 600 Jarvis Street, Room 219, Toronto, Ontario M4Y 2J6.

BREAD FOR THE WORLD, 207 East 16th Street, New York 10003, is a Christian citizens movement in the United States not specifically tied to any denomination. Its membership includes Catholic, Orthodox and conservative evangelical Protestants, as well as ecumenically oriented Protestants.

INTERRELIGIOUS TASK FORCE ON U.S. FOOD POLICY (National IMPACT), 110 Maryland Avenue, N.E., Washington, D.C. 20002. National IMPACT is primarily a coalition of denominational leaders concerned with legislative issues; hunger is one of those issues.

GATT-Fly, 11 Madison Avenue, Toronto, Ontario M5R 2S2 Canada. GATT-Fly is a project initiated by five Canadian churches (Anglican, Lutheran, Presbyterian, Roman Catholic and United Churches of Canada) to represent the interests of the Third World countries on issues of international trade and monetary reform.

CHAPTER 13
A NEW AGE IN HEALTH CARE *
R. NITA BARROW

Article 12
1. The States Parties to the present Covenant recognize the right of everyone to the *enjoyment of the highest attainable standard of physical and mental health*.
2. The steps to be taken by the States Parties to the present Covenant to achieve the full realization of this right shall include those necessary for:
(*a*) The provision for the reduction of the stillbirth-rate and of infant mortality and for the healthy development of the child;
(*b*) The improvement of all aspects of environmental and industrial hygiene;
(*c*) The prevention, treatment and control of epidemic, endemic, occupational and other diseases;
(*d*) The creation of conditions which would assure to all medical service and medical attention in the event of sickness.

International Covenant on Economic,
Social and Cultural Rights (Italics added)

A whole area of health care is presently undergoing close scrutiny, and relevant and available health care for all is being proposed as a target to be realized by the year 2000.

The irrelevance of the present health care model to the needs of the vast majority of the world's people has led to a search for alternative methods. In Western countries, where many of the models originated, there is growing dissatisfaction. This is verbalized mainly in reference to growing costs, the increased sophistication of the technology used, and the seemingly increasing dehumanization of the process.

In the largely rural populations of developing countries, where little or no services exist and where traditional methods no longer satisfy people's needs, innovative approaches have emerged. The major innovations common to some of the programs being conducted in these countries are examined in this article.

The real needs of the people are providing basic health services to those—largely the rural poor—who had no previous access to health care, and the fighting of common diseases with preventive means as opposed to curative medicine.

R. Nita Barrow is the director of the Christian Medical Commission, World Council of Churches, Geneva, Switzerland.
*Reprinted from the February 1978 issue of *response*.

Health care made available according to people's felt needs and on their own terms has involved full community acceptance, participation, and responsibility.

Experimentation both in selection and training of health workers has often been the answer to people's needs. Workers have been selected by the communities and trained to meet local needs. These are not highly trained professionals, but health workers whose preparation allows them to perform simple medical tasks and to teach the basics of disease prevention.

A multifaceted approach to development has emerged during the implementation of health care. The process has led to an examination of socioeconomic factors so that efforts to improve people's health should not be negated.

Three Innovative Programs

Three of the many health care programs where innovations have been made with success and where a developmental and nonelitist approach to Christian medical work has been tried are explored here. The people initiating them were dissatisfied with the available health care. The initiators, often from professional groups, recognized the importance of people's participation in their own health care.

The first program is the Comprehensive Rural

Health Project situated within a 10-mile radius of a village called Jamkhed in Maharashtra State, India. The area has a total population of 80,000 living in 55 villages. It is characterized by its strong caste system of which 50 percent are farmers, 20 percent untouchables, and the rest wealthy farmers and educated government employees who are the accepted leaders of the community.

The second is the Chimaltenango Development Project in Guatemala City. The Chimaltenango area encompasses 200,000 population. The majority are Indians.

The third is the Lardin Gabas Rural Health Project in northeastern Nigeria. Lardin Gabas—literally, eastern diocese—comprises an area of about 10,000 square miles and 900,000 people. More than 80 percent of this population of mostly subsistence farmers live in villages with average populations of 300-500. The project center is in Garkida.

Identification of Real Needs

Areas almost totally bereft of any health or other social services, or where those available were not used because of cost or lack of relevance to people's needs, were chosen as the sites for the programs. These areas had uniformly high rates of infant mortality and morbidity due to malnutrition and inadequate water supplies; low life expectancy; high rates of chronic diseases such as tuberculosis, leprosy, malaria, and parasitic diseases.

The Aroles family in Jamkhed, Carrol Behrhorst in Chimaltenango, and the Church of the Brethren team in Lardin Gabas each established a list of priorities reflecting these needs and proposing—with the involvement of local population—ways to meet them.

In Chimaltenango the project team realized the population needed other services besides health care. The following list of priorities was set: social justice, land tenure, population control, agricultural production and marketing, malnutrition solutions, health training and curative medicine.

Efforts were made to establish a central location or use an existing facility as a referral and training center such as the Garkida hospital in Lardin Gabas for diagnosis and emergency medical care. Sub-centers surrounding villages were also set up. Individual programs were then developed.

Response to People's Terms

In each program area the initiators spent much time traveling to different villages, and asking people,

"What do you think you need?" Often what the villagers identified as needs did not correspond to what the program team perceived them to be.

For example, in Jamkhed the team found that "very often, when talking to a doctor, the uppermost thinking in the villagers' minds is not health; the usual question is food." With the help of the program team, a village committee was formed which assumed the responsibility for collecting money for the purchase of fuel and utensils, for cooking food, for maintaining daily records and for getting children together for a meal with milk or soybeans provided through the program team.

In a Chimaltenango mountain village, it became clear what this community felt it most needed were chickens and apples. The program team sent an agricultural extension worker to help with chicken houses, immunization of chickens, and planting of apple trees.

It became clear to the various teams that "when you help people on their own terms, you have no acceptance problems." The cooperation of villagers is assured in taking responsibility for the community's health care. Community health committees made concrete commitments in terms of organization, collection of money, or provision of services.

In Lardin Gabas, constructing and furnishing the village health post was the responsibility of the Village Health Committee. If all was not in order by the time village health workers completed their training, they had to return home without their initial supply of medicines and equipment. In Jamkhed the first responsibility of the village committee was to find accommodation not only for the program team but also for the health centers.

Experimentation in Selecting and Training Health Workers

In each program perhaps the most important responsibility of the community health committee was selecting persons for training as community health workers and seeing that they fulfill the obligations of their jobs. The main emphasis of the training was to provide the health worker with a knowledge of health education and the basics of disease prevention, while curative treatment was taught on a more limited scale.

A unique feature of the Lardin Gabas teaching program is its extensive use of parables, drama, songs, and riddles—the traditional methods of learning among people who still depend heavily on oral traditions. These techniques are used both in teaching the course and in teaching the villages. Teaching stories are constructed to include the traditional knowledge or belief and to move, through the means of the story, to an action which will help solve the problem.

In each of the programs, auxiliary and paramedical workers, village health workers, or health promoters were thus trained. An essential feature included also is the participation of local practitioners, school teachers, school children, traditional midwives, and indeed, the whole community in its own health care.

Training in, and practice of, treatment of ailments is done by symptoms, not by diagnosis. It has become clear that "even people with the most sophisticated training, with years in school—too often err in their interpretation of the symptoms to make the diagnosis.... Experience is that symptom treatment results in a diagnosis.... Experience is that symptom treatment results in a relatively low error in management, realizing that most medical problems are rather simple and, with nature's help, actually heal themselves."

In the Lardin Gabas training, clinical teaching is limited to the most common symptoms, the disease that causes them, and the way it is contracted, with heavy emphasis on prevention through changing health practices.

A necessary component in the success of these programs lies in the careful supervision of each health worker. Rather different from the case for the average medical practitioner. In the Chimaltenango and Lardin Gabas programs, this supervision is done by requiring regular attendance at clinical training sessions; regular examinations; regular visits by the supervisor to the health worker's site; and regular reports from the local community health committee about the health worker's task, its quality, acceptance and the fees charged.

A Multifaceted Approach to Development

In all three programs, the careful inquiry into the felt needs of the people has led its initiators to formulate conclusions about the underlying causes of health problems and their interrelatedness to other socio-economic problems. For example, in Jamkhed it was obvious that leprosy was a social as well as a medical problem.

It was, therefore, necessary to attempt to break down social barriers by having leprosy patients attend the same clinic visited by other patients. At the same time that the medical team—composed of nurse, auxiliary nurse-midwife, family planning worker, basic health worker and laboratory technician—surveyed for leprosy, they also checked households for other health problems.

In Chimaltenango it was found that a high incidence of tuberculosis was related to maldistribution of land in a land tenure system. Tuberculosis, one disease of poverty, stems primarily from poor diet and crowded living conditions. Some of the local Indian population had to "go down to the south coast to work on coffee plantations. They would be away for three or four months at a time and be exposed to diseases they had never been exposed to before. They would return home half-sick and spend all the money they had made in trying to get well again. The only way we could help them was to give them loans in order to buy a small piece of land for themselves."

Again in Jamkhed, after encouraging the community to initiate a supplementary feeding program for children under five, the food being provided by outside gifts, the community was asked to seek a permanent solution to the problem of malnutrition. Thus encouraged, the village health committee decided to have a well sunk to irrigate land to grow enough nourishing food to solve the problem of undernourished children.

The committee decided which farmers were likely to have water in their fields, and would be generous after they had got the wells sunk in their land. Then the program team translated this community action into a scientific action.

In Lardin Gabas the long-term plan called for the intensification of services relating to nutrition, sanitation, wells, and hygiene.

It has become evident that health care in such communities means an orientation toward total community services. The practice of medicine is only a small part of the total pattern, which includes responding to total community needs whether they are in the field of agriculture, marketing, housing, home crafts, nutrition, planning, schooling or transport.

These health concepts used by a minority of people have begun to attract the attention of international agencies long concerned with the health of the nations of the world. The enunciation by the World Health Organization of Primary Health Care as one of the means of achieving health care for all by the year 2000 is an affirmation of this conviction.

The Church's role has been a significant part of the health care system of many countries. The Church pioneered in systems now considered nonrelevant in some areas. It also supports innovations that make it possible for people to participate and for the Church to be instrumental in helping develop new solutions to problems.

Questions for Reflection

1. Do citizens of the United States and Canada enjoy the "highest attainable standard of physical and mental health"? (See Article 12 at the beginning of this chapter.)

2. Do you believe that the State is responsible for the physical and mental health of its citizens?

3. Would you add any steps (see #2 of Article 12 of the Covenant) to achieve the full realization of this right?

4. Does your community have any of the problems described in this chapter?

5. "Health care made available according to people's felt needs and on their own terms has involved full community acceptance, participation, and responsibility," writes Nita Barrow. Is this the way health care is made available in our communities? Should this be the way? How would we go about it?

Exercises for Reflection

1. Relate this chapter to the introduction to Section III. In addition, reflect on the influence health care systems in the United States and Canada have had and continue to have in other countries—particularly in Asia, Africa and Latin America. Evaluate that influence. What other institutions in the Western countries have affected the health care of people in Asia, Africa, and Latin America?

2. In September 1978 an International Conference on Primary Health Care co-sponsored by WHO and UNICEF was held in the Soviet Union. Primary Health Care is defined as "essential health care universally accessible to individuals and families in the community, by means acceptable to them, through their full participation, and at a cost that the community can afford."[1] How did the United States and Canada participate in this conference? What were their statements? What implications do you see for the U.S. and Canada?

3. On October 10, 1978, an article appeared in *City News* in New York City. It was a report on hearings before the Health Subcommittee of the United States Senate (headed by Senator Edward Kennedy from Massachusetts). The discussion was on Senator Kennedy's national health insurance proposal. One woman said that medical costs had eaten up her family's

savings and "I am now sentenced to live in extreme poverty." A Canadian woman testified that "no one in Canada has to bear the mental strain and fear of massive medical expenses" since her country now has a national health insurance program.

> a. What is the National Health Insurance Program like in Canada? What problems are there? What advantages?
>
> b. Can the United States learn from the Canadian experience? What alternatives are there?
>
> c. What role should the Church play?

Preparing for Effective Witness: Further Reading

"To Promote the General Welfare," Chapter 9.

"To Ensure Availability of Food for All," Chapter 12.

Resources

United States citizens should check with Senator Edward Kennedy's office to find out what progress has been made by his subcommittee.

Health: A Time for Justice—on Primary Health Care. Published by the Public Information Division, World Health Organization, Geneva, June 1978. Available from UNICEF, United Nations, New York 10017.

Films

"Health Begins At Home"—1973 cartoon on family health—10 minutes, no commentary, color. Produced by Soiuzmultfilm, Moscow. Available for both U.S. and Canada from Alcoholism Research Information Center, P. O. Box 1207, Arlington, Va. 22210.

"Out of the Ivory Tower"—A 1977 film on education and training in medical schools. This film shows how a medical school in Rajasthan, India, has tackled the health problems of communities by making service to the community a regular part of its curriculum. 10 minutes—color. Produced by The Division of Public Information, World Health organization, Geneva. Available from the Alcoholism Research Information Center, P.O. Box 1207, Arlington, Va. 22210.

---

1. Information Bulletin from the Divisions of Public Information: WHO, Geneva, UNICEF, New York—PHC/4—Aug. 31, 1978.

CHAPTER 14
FREEDOM OF MOVEMENT
GERHARD A. ELSTON

Article 12

1. Everyone lawfully within the territory of a State shall, within that territory, have the right to *liberty of movement* **and freedom to choose his (her) residence.**

2. Everyone shall be *free to leave any country,* **including his (her) own.**

3. The above-mentioned rights shall not be subject to any restrictions except those which are provided by law, are necessary to protect national security, public order, public health or morals or the rights and freedoms of others, and are consistent with the other rights recognized in the present Covenant.

4. No one shall be arbitrarily deprived of the right to enter his (her) country.

International Covenant on Civil and
Political Rights (Italics added)

Nothing should be simpler and more uncontroversial than the freedom to travel. Included in the Universal Declaration of Human Rights, it is set forth in slightly greater detail in Article 12 of the International Convention on Civil and Political Rights.

Three separate rights are specified:

- The right to freedom of movement and choice of residence within the territory of any State for anyone lawfully within its borders.
- The freedom to leave any country, including one's own, and not to be arbitrarily deprived of the right to enter one's own country.
- The freedom to leave any country or to move within it, which "shall not be subject to any restrictions except those which are provided by law, are necessary to protect national security, public order, public health or morals or the rights and freedoms of others, and are consistent with the other rights recognized in the present Covenant."

In fact, the above rights are frequently abridged. Moreover, there are obstacles to freedom of movement which are not covered in the Covenant.

Gerhard Elston, now a U.S. citizen, was a teenage refugee from Hitler's Germany. He lived and traveled as a "stateless alien of former enemy nationality" on three continents—with difficulties and restrictions. He is presently Executive Director of Amnesty International U.S.A.

The most obvious of these is the fact that there is no established right to enter any country except your own. The averred right to leave any country is rather pointless if no other country will let you in, as many political refugees have had to learn to their cost and frustration. Indeed, any tourist will discover that the right to leave a country can end at the airline counter; if you present your ticket for a trip abroad but have failed to obtain a necessary visa for entry at your destination, you will not be allowed to board.

Tens of thousands among those who died in Nazi concentration camps had valid passports and exit permits—the Germans did not attempt to block the departure of many categories of people they deemed undesirable—but they were caught because no country would issue them an entry permit. Many who had crossed a border illegally were forcibly returned; many Soviet subjects were similarly "repatriated" against their will from other parts of Europe after World War II.

There now is a United Nations Protocol relating to the Status of Refugees (ratified by Canada and the United States, among others) which seeks, among other things, to prevent forcible return of persons to their territory of origin if they are likely to be persecuted there for political, religious or racial reasons. But because the laws of few countries are in full compliance with the minimum standards provided by that protocol (which itself leaves considerable gaps), expulsions and forced repatriations are still frequent occurrences. United States law and practice have never met those minimum standards. Canadian regulations—once more nearly in compliance—appear more restrictive since the recent changes in immigration legislation.

Entry visas, as well as residence and work permits, loom large in the lives of refugees and others who seek to change their country of residence. But there are other impediments.

Legally, to leave a country, including your own, a person normally must have a valid passport or other travel document and, frequently, an exit permit—or even permits from different government agencies. For instance, a paper showing that you have no tax-bill outstanding may be necessary. (Long-term foreign visitors to the United States have been required to obtain such a tax liability clearance document before departure.) Portugal, until a few years ago, required that Portuguese women traveling without either father or husband carry written authorization from husband or guardian, in addition to their passport, for each border crossing.

Normally, such documents can be routinely obtained, though it may be a time-consuming nuisance. But charters, bills, or covenants of rights are not required to protect persons under "normal" circumstances; clearly, such laws or declarations are intended to protect rights which are threatened. Unhappily, the very language of the Covenant articles makes it rather easy for states to curtail rather than safeguard the rights by indicating exceptions "provided by law" or "necessary to protect national security," to name only two.

On that basis, many countries have made possession of a passport a privilege rather than a right. Much publicity has been given to the difficulties encountered by members of the Jewish community in the Soviet Union who wish to emigrate. While those have been enormous and, in some individual cases, insurmountable, a fairly large number of exit permits and travel documents have actually been granted on a regular basis. That is noteworthy because it appears to be an exception rather than a rule. Most of the socialist countries of Eastern Europe, and many other states, do not issue passports to any of their citizens simply on demand. Some countries also restrict the use of a passport to particular trips or particular countries.

There was a time when certain United States citizens could not obtain passports for security reasons.

Until recently, U.S. passports were endorsed with limitations disallowing travel to certain socialist states, even though the restriction was not enforced due to a Supreme Court ruling assuring U.S. citizens the right to passport and free travel.

It is clear, however, that ratification of the Covenants would put the United States in a stronger position (much as Canada already holds) to argue for unrestricted freedom of movement between countries—a principle endorsed in the Helsinki agreements and elsewhere.

There are other problems. Some people have chosen exile over imprisonment. But what is "arbitrary" when you are deprived of the right to enter your own country? For that matter, what is your own country when you consider yourself a member of an ethnic or national group that does not have its own state or internationally recognized government or boundaries? Examples are all too plentiful: Kurds and Armenians, Cypriots from either side of the language line, Palestinians, Tibetans, South Africans, not to mention innumerable other groups of people, have at one time or another been deprived of the right to enter what they consider their own country. State authority will never regard its legal actions as "arbitrary," but clearly persons subject to exclusion or expulsion will so regard it, no matter how "legal" it may be.

Recourse seems to lie primarily in creating a new mood—a public will, a worldwide standard in such matters—to create pressures on states to live up to the letter and the spirit of such agreed-to rights.

That would also seem to apply to rights that are not yet embodied in the present covenants, such as stronger safeguards for those who have need to claim asylum—especially against deportation to countries where there is reason to fear for their safety.

Much of this is attainable, if only people cared enough. There will always be financial and other restrictions that keep the alleged right to move freely about this earth, and live where you like, unattainable by many. But if there is a right to medical care and a right to travel, then if your child, to survive, needs treatment only attainable halfway around the globe, that possibility should at least be a visionary dream for all people, however poor, in a world that takes the rights of all humans seriously.

While we strive for such a visionary goal, there are large numbers of more immediate infractions to correct. Many lives could be saved, many families reunited, many hurts healed if the freedom of movement as set forth as rights in the International Covenant on

Civil and Political Rights were to be respected by all nations. We should all work to create a public will toward that end.

Questions for Reflection

1. Do you believe all persons have a right to travel across international borders, or within their country? Would there be any person to whom you would refuse entry into your country? Why?

2. Do you believe everyone has a right to emigrate? To live and work or study anywhere? Within one's country? Or in any country? Explain.

3. Would you favor open immigration? Would you favor permanent legal residence for people currently in the United States or Canada illegally (i.e., without proper permanent immigration visa or parole number or "landed immigrant" status)? Explain your response.

4. Do you believe the United States and Canada should waive visa requirements for short-term visitors? Students? All immigrants? Why? Why not?

5. Do you believe that Canada and the United States should pressure other governments to waive visa restrictions, emigration or other travel restrictions? Explain.

Preparing for Effective Witness: Further Reading

"Aliens," Chapter 4.
"Migrant Labour—The Breaking of Families," Chapter 2.

Exercises for Reflection

1. Many events in biblical history involved questions of immigration, emigration and exile. Some of the same issues were prevalent then as well as now. Why did the Israelites come into Egypt? Why did they leave? Why was it difficult for them to leave? (See Genesis 42-50 and Exodus 1-15.) Read the Book of Ruth. Why did Naomi and her husband go to the Moabite country? How was Ruth the Moabitess, a foreigner, treated when she went to Bethlehem with her mother-in-law?

Why did Jesus and his family seek refuge in Egypt when he was a child? (See Matthew 2:1-23.) What other stories could you point to? Are they helpful or do they simply suggest similarities in our problems?

2. "Few nations openly oppose the ideals of human rights, yet over the past two decades much more attention has been given to the splinter in the eye of the other than to the log in one's own..." writes Dwain Epps in the introduction to Section III. In what way does this sentence apply to the United States and Canada in relation to "freedom of movement"?

3. Reread the entire Introduction to Section III. In what way can we deal with our own problems in relation to "freedom of movement"? In what way can we support our brothers and sisters in other lands in their similar efforts?

CHAPTER 15
THE MOST DISCRIMINATORY SENTENCE
TOM WICKER

Article 6

1. Every human being has the inherent *right to life*. This right shall be protected by law. No one shall be arbitrarily deprived of his (her) life.

2. In countries which have not abolished the *death penalty,* sentence of death may be imposed *only for the most serious crimes* in accordance with the law in force at the time of the commission of the crime and not contrary to the provisions of the present Covenant and to the Convention on the Prevention and Punishment of the Crime of Genocide. This penalty can only be carried out pursuant to a final judgement rendered by a competent court.

3. When deprivation of life constitutes the crime of genocide, it is understood that nothing in this article shall authorize any State Party to the present Covenant to derogate in any way from any obligation assumed under the provisions of the Convention on the Prevention and Punishment of the Crime of Genocide.

4. Anyone sentenced to death shall have the right to seek pardon or commutation of the sentence. Amnesty, pardon or commutation of the sentence of death may be granted in all cases.

5. Sentence of *death shall not be imposed* for crimes committed by persons *below eighteen years* of age and shall not be carried out on *pregnant women.*

6. Nothing in this article shall be invoked to delay or to prevent the abolition of capital punishment by any State Party to the present Covenant.

*International Covenant on Civil
and Political Rights* (Italics added)

The death penalty, capital punishment, is the most discriminatory sentence levied by the courts in America. It is most discriminatory against black people. Of the 3,859 people executed in this country between 1930 and 1968, 53.5 percent were black.

It's discriminatory against the poor. The Furman decision in 1972 tried to remove some of the caprice and arbitrariness in the death penalty. But even after that, of all the persons on death row two years later, 60 percent had been unemployed at the time of their having committed a crime, 62 percent were unskilled

This article was excerpted from a speech given by Tom Wicker, Associate Editor of *The New York Times,* during an April 1977 Witness Against Executions in Atlanta, Georgia. It is reprinted here from Engage/Social Action, June, 1977, © e/sa.

servants or domestic workers, 50 percent had never completed high school and over 90 percent had to be represented in court by appointed counsel.

It's one of the few things in the world that may be discriminatory against males. Of all those 3,859 people executed in thirty-eight years, only thirty-two were women.

The death penalty is also discriminatory as to the region of the country. Georgia has executed the most people since statistics began to be kept in 1930. However, of the first ten states that have executed the most people in those thirty-eight years, six of them are southern. My home state of North Carolina is third only to Georgia and Texas with 263 people executed.

Some people, however, insisted that the death penalty, however cruel it may be and however difficult or even discriminatory, deters crime. The death penalty does not deter crime. The statistics are available to prove that fact. Those statistics show that states that have abolished the death penalty have seen no increase in homicides. Statistics show that states that have abolished the death penalty and then reinstituted it, have shown no drop in homicide—some have, in fact, shown an increase.

Death penalty states as a group have no lower rate of homicide. In fact, in the years 1928 through 1949, the rates of homicide were higher in states that executed people for murder. Everybody who knows anything about criminal justice realizes that any form of sentencing to deter crime must be swift and sure and no penalty in the courts today is less swift and less sure than the death penalty, and therefore less a deterrent to crime. Some proponents of capital punishment say the public insists on it. The public, though, doesn't really insist on the execution of people. I know all the arguments. I know about the thirty-five states whose legislatures passed some form of death penalty law after the Furman case. I know about all these polls that say people favor the death penalty. But I'm only interested in facts.

Facts show that from the peak year of 1935, when we executed a total of 199 people, there has been a steady downtrend, without a break. In the 1950s it fell below 100; in 1961 only 42 were executed; and it fell below 25 in 1963. Then from 1967 until early this year there were no executions. Now that is the only poll that counts.

The people of the country may have the death penalty on the books, to proclaim some persons not fit to live, but modern American people do not want executions. I believe that those who insist on carrying out executions are going to find that the American people will not put up with executions.

However, those of us opposed to the death penalty are obligated, in making our case, to deal with the realities. Those realities are that this country and its great cities are paralyzed with fear of crime. Out of that fear of crime come the pressures for capital punishment.

That fear is very justified because we have more violent crime than any Western society. Therefore, those of us against the death penalty have an obligation to speak to the facts of so much crime in America. If we say the death penalty will do nothing about lessening crime, then what will?

I know one thing: people—ordinary citizens, district attorneys, members of Congress, U.S. Presidents—are fooling themselves if they believe shortcuts like the death penalty will diminish crime in this country. They are fooling themselves if they believe we can diminish crime by shortcutting the constitutional rights of American people. They are fooling themselves if they think we have a lot of crime in this country only because judges are soft and are coddling criminals. Above all, they are fooling themselves if they think we can really do something about crime by putting more people in the barbaric prisons of America, and keeping them there longer.

Reasons for Crime

Why do we have so much crime? Nobody knows for sure, but I think we have so much crime for a number of reasons.

We have so much crime because we have so much economic injustice, because we have so many poor people living side by side with so much affluence. Poor people know there are a lot of people who've got what they haven't got.

We have so much crime in this country because of a vast and unconscionable rate of unemployment, above 7 percent. Seven percent unemployment means something like 40 percent unemployment among blacks and teenagers. And 40 percent unemployment among black teenagers, at the rate of economic recovery scheduled today by this administration, means that more than one-third of the black teenagers in America are never going to have a job because by the time they are twenty-one, they are going to be lost to crime, prisons, drug addiction, welfare, or any number of ways.

We have crime in America today because there is so much racial injustice and so much social injustice. We have bad housing, bad schools that don't teach, poor nutrition, too little health care that costs too much.

We have crime in this country because we have so much legal injustice. We have too many police who believe it's their job to control the poor people and the black people and to protect the privileged. We have a legal system that works for the affluent and the rich rather than for the poor. We have overcrowded, insensitive courts administering all the arbitrary laws. We have prisons that are no more than poor houses for unwanted lives and schools for crime in retaliation upon society that has sent people to prison in the name of rehabilitation. We have a criminal justice system that from beginning to end is shot full with arbitrariness and unfairness—over decisions of arrests, charges, bail, trial, sentencing, imprisonment, and parole.

We have too much crime in America because we have a political system that is fundamentally designed and dedicated to the maintenance of the status quo and the protection of privilege.

We just can't say we're against the death penalty. We've got to recognize that the question goes far deeper than that. We are not going to win this battle until we have economic, political, and social institutions that work to the end of generosity to the weak and justice to the disadvantaged.

Questions for Discussion

1. What is your reaction to Tom Wicker's position on the death penalty? List your agreements and your disagreements.

2. What are the theological/biblical rationales for or against the death penalty?

3. What is your own position on the death penalty? How do you justify your position? Write it out.

Exercises for Reflection

The United Nations through both the General Assembly and the Economic and Social Council has established that the main objective to be pursued in the field of capital punishment is that of progressively restricting the number of offenses for which the death penalty may be imposed with a view to the desirability of abolishing this punishment. (United Nations General Assembly Resolution 32/61, adopted Dec. 8, 1977.)

1. Where do the United States and Canada stand on the issue of capital punishment? Describe.

2. How strong an issue is it in the U.S. and Canada? In the same United Nations General Assembly Resolution (32/61) it was agreed "to consider, with high priority, at its thirty-fifth session (1980) the question of capital punishment."

3. Where do our denominations stand on the issue of capital punishment? Should we influence our governments' participation on this issue in the 35th Session of the UN General Assembly in 1980?

4. "Every human being has the inherent right to life. This right shall be protected by law. No one shall be arbitrarily deprived of his (her) life." (See Article 6, #1 at the beginning of this chapter.) In *Paradox and Promise in Human Rights,* Peggy Billings suggests (Chapter 2, pp. 44-47) that as a justice of the International Court of Justice, you hear the case of "The Families of Mark Clark and Fred Hampton vs. The

Chicago Police and the FBI." What would be your verdict?

5. "When deprivation of life constitutes the crime of genocide ..." (see Article 6, #3 at the beginning of this chapter). Canada has ratified the Convention on the Prevention and Punishment of the Crime of Genocide but the United States has only signed it and it is still pending in the U.S. Senate. This convention has been proposed for signature and ratification since December 9, 1948. Why is the United States finding it so difficult to ratify it? As of August 1978, 82 nations had ratified. U.S. citizens may wish to pressure for ratification of this Convention.

6. In *Paradox and Promise in Human Rights* Peggy Billings suggests (Chapter 2, pp. 40-42) that as a justice of the International Court of Justice you hear the case of "Antonio Millape, Mapuche Confederation vs. The Government of Chile." The charge is *genocide.* What would be your verdict?

7. Relate this chapter to the Introduction to Section III.

Preparing for Effective Witness: Further Reading

"To Transform Systems Dealing With Conflicts and Crimes," Chapter 11.

"A Charter for Racial Justice Policies in an Interdependent Global Community," Chapter 6.

CHAPTER 16
INTERNATIONAL YEAR OF THE CHILD 1979
MIA ADJALI

Article 24

1. *Every child* shall have, without any discrimination as to race, colour, sex, language, religion, national or social origin, property or birth, the *right to such measures of protection* as are required by his (her) status as a minor, on the part of his (her) family, society and the State.

2. Every child shall be *registered immediately after birth* and shall *have a name.*

3. Every child has the *right to acquire a nationality.*

International Covenant on
Civil and Political Rights (Italics added)

International Year of the Child 1979

The year 1979 has been proclaimed by the United Nations as the "International Year of the Child." The official logo was designed by Erik Jerichau of Denmark. Surrounded by the UN laurel leaves are two embracing figures, symbolizing the relationship between adult and child. The year 1979 is when The United Nations Declaration of the Rights of the Child will be 20 years old. It affirms:

The right to affection, love and understanding.
The right to adequate nutrition and medical care.
The right to free education.
The right to full opportunity for play and recreation.
The right to a name and nationality.
The right to special care, if handicapped.
The right to be among the first to receive relief in times of disaster.
The right to be a useful member of society and to develop individual abilities.
The right to be brought up in a spirit of peace and universal brotherhood.
The right to enjoy these rights, regardless of race, color, sex, religion, national or social origin.

The year 1979 is the time when people throughout the world will together strive to discover the best ways and means to alert their societies to the needs of children. A short pamphlet distributed by the U.S. Committee for UNICEF quickly outlines the reasons for and the goals of International Year of the Child.

Why an International Year of the Child?

For one and a half billion reasons—most of them under ten years old.

Because all children have special needs—but in many cases these needs are not being adequately met.

Because children are our future—and our most precious resource. The quality of tomorrow's world—perhaps even its survival—will be determined by the well-being, safety and development of children today.

Because children are wholly dependent upon adults—and we owe them the best we have to give.

What Is IYC?

An opportunity to focus on children, and put them in their proper place: at the centre of world concern.

Twentieth anniversary of the United Nations Declaration of the Rights of the Child: a time to recall its principles and redouble our efforts to put them into practice.

A year supported by all members of the

United Nations to promote lasting action to improve the lives of children everywhere.

A time for governments, organizations and individuals to work together in concrete, constructive, practical programmes for the benefit of children.

What Can I Do?

Look around. Listen. Learn. And act.

What are main needs of children in your neighborhood? Your town? Your country? The world beyond?

What are your own major interests? Special skills and opportunities?

Talk to friends and neighbors about IYC. Start a discussion group. Write to editors, try to influence legislators in defence of children and their rights. Help to raise funds for better services for children at home and if possible, abroad. Offer your time and talents.

Care, and get involved.

In both the United States and in Canada there are National Commissions for the International Year of the Child:

> National Commission for I.Y.C.—
> U.S.A.
> 600 E Street, N.W., Fifth Floor
> Washington, D.C. 20435
>
> Canadian Commission for I.Y.C.—
> Canada
> 323 Chapel Street
> Ottawa, Ontario KIN   7Z2, Canada

In each country there are Committees for UNICEF:

United States:U.S. Committee for UNICEF
331 East 38th Street
New York, New York 10016

Canada: UNICEF Canada
443 Mount Pleasant Road
Toronto, Ontario, Canada M4S 2L8

Get in touch with these organizations. Find out how you can get involved. Perhaps your churches have already made plans.... Find out. In 1977, the United Presbyterian Church, USA, and the Presbyterian Church, U.S., published a special issue of their magazine *Church and Society* entitled "On Being A Child: An Inquiry Into the Needs and Rights of Children and the Commission of the Church." In the foreword, Dr. Thelma Adair, Professor of Education at Queens University, exhorts the readers to proclaim the present century as the century of the child.

At this point in the decade of the seventies, there is a constellation of new information and heightened interest concerning the needs and rights of children. Our understanding and knowledge of growth and development, expanding learning experience, increased opportunity for health care, and technology to provide for basic human needs, has grown manyfold. From previous generations we have inherited an ongoing, espoused concern for children. Today, with the use of powerful, critical tools of science and rational, logical analysis, we have the capability to plan and achieve the monumental task of providing the good life for all children.

Public and private groups at all levels are taking a new look at their roles and responses on behalf of children. The church, too, is and must be involved in this effort. Data from many disciplines reaffirm that the basic tenets of our Judeo-Christian beliefs—the worth and dignity of persons, especially children—are indispensable to a healthy, viable community. Christians have a mandate to value the child. Jesus said, "Let the children come unto me for such is the kingdom of heaven.... If anyone causes one of these little ones who believes in me to sin, it would be better for him to have a large millstone hung around his neck and to be drowned in the depths of the sea."

What does the record show? Little can be achieved by arguing about what has been done, what is being done, or what could be done. The task of conceptualizing, developing, and implementing relevant practical response should be given high priority by the church. All have professed compassion and concern for children, their needs and their rights, but again and again the record reveals rhetoric, platitudes, and exhortations. There is little evidence of commitment of vast resources and sustained positive, massive and constructive action. There must be greater commitment to and effort toward the things in which we believe. There must be the will to act and the courage to show care and concern.

It is imperative that we act now to accelerate the pace and rate of change. For children there can be no further delay in providing optimum conditions for the fulfillment of human potential. The future of the child is now. The opportunity for our time to become the century of the child rests with us. We, the adults, are the keepers of the future. We can choose to continue to be a part of the problem or choose to become keys to the solution. Clearly our task is to face the harsh realities of the moment, affirm the rights and needs of every child, and accept the responsibility of our stewardship to children of the world.

Those who have contributed to this volume provided the widest spectrum of advocates for children. They have selflessly attended to the task of searching for alternatives and solutions to facilitate the best possible life for each child at every stage of growth and development. The church must continue this search for ways of raising the levels of consciousness, to heighten the degree of informed awareness, and to support and undergird the efforts that would enable each child to become an inheritor of the kingdom.

Thelma Adair
Foreword, *On Being A Child**

The International Year of the Child is a worldwide effort. As we wrestle with our problems at home, we join the same struggle of people everywhere. Perhaps the answers to all the needs of children will not be found but perhaps the right questions will be raised. (Introduction, Section III)

Preparing for Effective Witness: Further Reading
"To Promote the General Welfare," Chapter 9.

Resources
International Year of the Child and the World Council of Churches, report of the World Council of Churches Task Force on the I.Y.C. as endorsed by the WCC Executive Committee, February 1978. World Council of Churches, Programme Unit on Education and Renewal, Sub-unit on Education, 150 route de Ferney, 1211 Geneva 20, Switzerland.

UNICEF Information Bulletin, Information Division of UNICEF, United Nations, New York, New York 10017.

UNICEF News, published four times a year by UNICEF Information Division, United Nations, New York 10017.

---

* Copies of this study are available from *Church & Society*, Room 1244K, 475 Riverside Drive, New York, New York 10027. ($1.00 per copy; 75¢ each for 50-100 copies; 60¢ each for 100 or more)

CHAPTER 17
EXPRESSION-PROPAGANDA-
ASSEMBLY-ASSOCIATION
MARY LITELL

Article 17

1. No one shall be subjected to *arbitrary or unlawful interference* with his (her) *privacy, family, home or correspondence,* nor to unlawful attacks on his (her) *honour and reputation.*

2. Everyone has the right to the protection of the law against such interference or attacks.

Article 18

1. Everyone shall have the *right to freedom of thought, conscience and religion.* This right shall include *freedom to have or to adopt a religion or belief* of his (her) choice, and freedom, either individually or in community with others and in public or private, *to manifest his (her) religion or belief in worship, observance, practice and teaching.*

2. No one shall be subject to coercion which would impair his (her) freedom to have or to adopt a religion or belief of his (her) choice.

3. Freedom to manifest one's religion or beliefs may be subject only to such limitations as are prescribed by law and are necessary to protect public safety, order, health, or morals or the fundamental rights and freedoms of others.

4. The States Parties to the present Covenant undertake to have respect for the *liberty of parents* and, when applicable, legal guardians to ensure the *religious and moral education of their children* in conformity with their own convictions.

Article 19

1. Everyone shall have the right to hold opinions without interference.

2. Everyone shall have the *right to freedom of expression;* this right shall include *freedom to seek, receive and impart information* and ideas of all kinds, regardless of frontiers, either orally, in writing or in print, in the form of art, or through any other media of his (her) choice.

3. The exercise of the rights provided for in paragraph 2 of this article *carries with it special duties and responsibilities.* It may therefore be subject to certain restrictions, but these shall only be such as are provided by law and are necessary:

   (a) For respect of the *rights or reputations* of others;

   (b) For the *protection of national security or of public order,* or of *public health or morals.*

Article 20

1. Any propaganda for war shall be prohibited by law.

2. Any advocacy of national, racial, or religious hatred that constitutes incitement to discrimination, hostility or violence shall be prohibited by law.

Article 21

The right of peaceful assembly shall be recognized. No restrictions may be placed on the exercise of this right other than those imposed in conformity with the law and which are necessary in a democratic society in the interests of national security in public safety, public order, the protection of public health or morals or the protection of the rights and freedoms of others.

Article 22

1. Everyone shall have the right to *freedom of association with others,* including the *right to form and join trade unions* for the protection of his (her) interests.

2. No restrictions may be placed on the exercise of this right other than those which are prescribed by law and which are necessary in a democratic society in the interests of national security or public safety, public order, the protection of public health or morals or the protection of the rights and freedoms of others. This article *shall not prevent the imposition of lawful restrictions on members of the armed forces and of the police in their exercise of this right.*

3. Nothing in this article shall authorize States Parties to the International Labour Organisation Convention of 1948 concerning Freedom of Association and Protection of the Right to Organize to take legislative measures which would prejudice the guarantees provided for in that Convention.

International Covenant on Civil
and Political Rights (Italics added)

"...We have discussed so many times what is just, what is right with regard to land and wealth. But I think we don't sufficiently appreciate the fact that right without might is not enough. They must go together. The power of principle cannot stand on its own. It must be accompanied by the principle of power."

"If you have right, but don't have might," asks Mang Henio, "what are you? You are only a 'boy scout.' The powers-that-be will not take you seriously.... But if you have right and might," Mang Henio grins almost mischievously, "what are you? You are like the Viet Cong! Before you know it the powers-that-be will want to negotiate with you."

"It is not enough to be innocent like doves, Christ told us. We must be clever and wise as serpents" (Matt. 10:16).

"Even John the Baptist had some power when he was languishing in jail. The Bible says Herod would not put him to death because he was afraid of the people. John apparently had a mass base or following. But of course," Mang Henio is grinning again, "of course the dance of Salome was a miscalculation..."[1] (Matt. 14:1-11).

* * *

Mang Henio lives in the Philippines. Would he and his friends have had this discussion if they lived in the United States of America?

Their discussion expresses in a very concrete manner a crucial point of the preamble to the International

---

Mary Litell is correspondent for International Study Days, an education project on justice and domination. She is also a Franciscan sister living in Redwood City, California.

1. *Peasant Theology,* reported by Charlie Avila. This book, an excellent example of grass roots groups doing theology from their own experience, is now out of print. World Student Christian Federation is planning to publish an expanded second edition.

Covenant on Civil and Political Rights: "The ideal of free human beings enjoying civil and political freedom and freedom from fear and want can only be achieved if conditions are created whereby everyone may enjoy his (her) civil and political rights, as well as his (her) economic, social and cultural rights." In other words, "rights" are only one part of the means toward full human freedom. By themselves, these rights are empty promises.

The message of Jesus Christ urges us to move even farther in our understanding of relationships among people. Christ calls us to a life of love. In love there are no rights, for love is a gift, freely given. It is only little by little, however, that we learn to love. Thus the concept of rights becomes helpful as a step toward an ideal human order. Further, this concept is not only helpful, but also necessary, as a minimal basis for cooperation within and among nations of such diverse economic, political and cultural systems. As expressed in the UN Covenants, then, rights are not an end in themselves; rather they are one of the necessary means toward a rich human climate in which we can learn to truly love one another in full human freedom.

The following reflection on the traditional civil liberties is set in the context of these two basic considerations: rights become effective when they are accompanied by substance, or "might," and when they are understood not as ends in themselves, but as one means by which we can build up the fully human community.

For nearly two hundred years, the Constitution of the United States has guaranteed most of the formal rights expressed in Articles 17-22 of the UN Covenant on Civil and Political Rights:

The right to privacy;
The right to freedom of thought, conscience, religion;
The right to freedom of expression;
The right to assemble peacefully;
The right to freedom of association with others.

The UN Covenant includes as basic to the right of free association the right to form and join trade unions for the protection of interests. It also lists, among these rights, a strong injunction: propaganda for war shall be prohibited by law, and advocacy of national, racial or religious hatred that incites discrimination, hostility or violence shall be prohibited by law.

Is there any need to enter into a covenant with other nations that will bind us to honor these rights? Does our society fully enjoy these rights? If we ratify such a covenant, who will—who can—effectively assure these rights? The state? The people? Reflections on a few well-known situations experienced in our society may help us to understand more fully the intent and spirit of the International Covenant on Civil and Political Rights.

I. During the late sixties and early seventies, hundreds of thousands of Americans in the United States exercised their right of free expression and free assembly. They marched in the streets; they gathered in parks, churches, town halls, on campuses, publicly expressing their disagreement with U.S. intervention in Vietnam. Many of those protesters were jailed; more of them were kept under surveillance. Phones were tapped, homes and offices were searched. In 1978 we are still being informed of violations of privacy, of provocations to riot performed in those years by agencies of our government.

During this same period some of these same government agencies, in cooperation with U.S. corporations, were violating the civil rights of the people of Chile. These violations were largely unknown at that time to the people on whose "behalf" they were committed.

Congressional investigations of violations of rights in both these situations were held and publicized. Some persons involved in the violations have been, or are now being, prosecuted. Yet the House of Representatives is currently considering passage of a bill— H.R. 6869—which will legalize many of the means that were used in these situations to deny the rights of privacy, association, expression and assembly. The Senate has already passed its own version—S. 1437— of this same bill.[2]

1. Where does all this leave us?
2. Whose rights were violated, whose were protected in the situations described above? Why?
3. Were any groups in our society working to protect the rights being violated?
4. If the state does not assure all its people the right to civil and political freedom, who can assure this right?

II. In the last few years we have read a great deal about charges that religious sects brainwash their young adherents. Parents have forcibly removed sons and daughters from such sects. They have employed private detectives to "kidnap" their sons and daughters and return them to their homes for "deprogram-

2. More information on this bill can be obtained from the National Committee Against Repressive Legislation, 510 C Street, N.E., Washington, D.C. 20002 and from the National Alliance Against Racism and Political Repression, 150 Fifth Avenue, N.Y.C. 10011.

ming." Several such cases have been brought to court. How can we understand the right to practice the religion of one's choice in these situations?

This question is difficult, for there are several aspects to consider:

1. What is meant by "freely choosing and practicing a religion or belief"?
2. What constitutes religion?
3. What constitutes brainwashing?
4. If a sect is truly harmful to its adherents, how can this be determined?
5. Some people have called for the banning of such sects. What consequences for religious freedom might such a precedent have?
6. Who can assure religious freedom in such cases?

III. Fred Harris, an independent candidate in the 1976 United States presidential campaign, withdrew from the race charging lack of access to the media. We are well aware of the power of the media to shape public opinion. In whose interests is this power exercised?

Recently the Supreme Court ruled that a corporation is entitled to the same freedom of expression that an individual person enjoys. A major consequence in this decision is that corporation expenditures in their own independent efforts to influence electoral issues may not be limited. Such expenditures could be used, among other ways, to buy media coverage. A crucial question here is whether or not the spirit of the UN Covenant includes corporations as citizens.

Every year, in several cities, Nazis hold large public parades. These are covered by the local media and in some cases by national media. What is the spirit of the injunction against propaganda for war (Article 21)? Who has the power, or can assume the power, to enforce this injunction? Does this injunction infringe upon the rights of free speech and assembly? If so, is the infringement justified?

Further important questions in regard to these situations would be:

1. In a society dependent on mass media for broad dissemination of opinions, what are the responsibilities of the media?
2. Can the mass media, structured as they are now, allow all citizens equal right to expression?
3. Do the practices of media, or the federal regulations of these practices, promote equal access to free expression?

IV. In the United States and throughout the world a movement is beginning among workers toward full participation in their own unions. This movement reflects a much broader aim among peoples who are seeking fuller participation in the various institutions that affect their lives. One example of this movement among workers is the struggle of cannery workers in northern California. These cannery workers are represented by the teamsters union. They have complained that much of their dues goes directly into pension funds over which they have no control; that though the majority of cannery workers are Spanish-speaking, they have not been permitted to hold their meetings in Spanish, or print their bylaws in Spanish; that elections are held in places or at times that are inaccessible to most of the workers. These and other instances of the denial of the right to freely associate in their own union have been brought to court or to the National Labor Relations Board. Cannery workers have lost many of the decisions.

1. Does the right of association, as expressed in the UN Covenant, have a relationship to the growing movement for full participation in institutions that affect the lives of people?
2. Do our public laws promote or suppress the right of association?
3. What groups in our society are actively promoting this right in the areas of labor? Of education? Of health care? Of government?

In Stearns, Kentucky, 150 miners have been on strike for nearly two years. They are striking for the right to organize as a local of United Mine Workers of America. The circuit court, as well as the National Labor Relations Board, has more often decided in favor of the company that refuses to bargain with the United Mine Workers of America than in favor of the miners. The company in question has a poor safety record, with repeated violations of federal safety regulations. The strike was begun in an effort to obtain safe working conditions. This struggle of workers to organize is only one of many in the South. Throughout the country, less than one quarter of the workforce is organized.

1. What is the spirit of the right of free association (Article 22) in the UN Covenant?
2. Do our public laws and regulations promote or suppress this right?
3. What groups in our society are actively promoting this right?
4. Are these groups working in cooperation with one another? What obstacles do they face?

Exploration of the situations described above is only

a beginning in the understanding of those rights we have traditionally called civil liberties. It would be interesting to image, together, a society where these rights were fully understood and lived. Then, letting the image continue, imagine the people of such a society learning to live freely, in a love-gift relationship with one another. Would there be differences in these two phases of that utopian society? Are there concrete steps we can take today toward the building up of such a society?

Preparing for Effective Witness: Further Reading

"To Secure a Correction of Abuses," Chapter 8.

"A Charter for Racial Justice Policies in an Interdependent Global Community," Chapter 6.

"The Recent Struggle," Chapter 4, pp. 75-78 in *Paradox and Promise in Human Rights* by Peggy Billings.

Exercises for Reflection

In *Paradox and Promise in Human Rights,* Peggy Billings suggests (Chapter 2, pp. 47-50) that as a justice of the International Court of Justice, you hear the case of "The People vs. the Shah of Iran." What would be your verdict?

Relate this chapter to the introduction of Section I: "We understand the Gospel to call individuals into the whole—there to be instruments of humanization, liberation and change."

Relate this chapter to the introduction of Section II: "The fact is that human relations are largely governed by the distribution of power in society."

Relate this chapter to the introduction of Section III: "Few nations openly oppose the ideals of human rights, yet over the past decades much more attention has been given to the splinter in the eye of the other than the log in one's own...."

The final questions are:

a. How will we become instruments of humanization?

b. How will we assure that power is distributed justly in our societies?

c. How will we wrestle with our own problems and strive to support our brothers and sisters in other lands?

REFLECTIONS ON SECTION III

UNIVERSAL HUMAN RIGHTS APPLY TO OUR
OWN SITUATION
AS WELL AS TO OTHERS

Understanding The Need For
Solidarity

The Preamble to both Human Rights Covenants ends by noting that "the individual, having duties to other individuals and to the community to which he (she) belongs, is under a responsibility to strive for the promotion and observance of the rights recognized in the present Covenant(s)." The mandate "Love your neighbor" is thus an international assumption which calls for the solidarity of all people in the struggles and responsibilities for implementing the International Covenants on Human Rights.

Solidarity is defined as "complete unity, as of opinion, purpose, interest, feeling, etc...." (Webster) Christians prefer to talk about "the community of believers" or "the Christian Fellowship." It is difficult for us to even think about acting in solidarity with people outside that "Christian community." We sometimes fail to imagine a "unity of opinion, purpose, interest or feeling" with people outside that community. Reverend Gilbert H. Caldwell, chaplain of the University of Massachusetts at Amherst, suggests that Christians have a tendency to protect and segregate the Christian Gospel from certain perspectives as though it were too vulnerable—as though Christians did not believe in the power of that Gospel.[1] Isn't it possible to act with people of other faiths, of other beliefs, other ideologies? Jesus said, "If you love only those who love you, what reward can you expect? Surely the tax-gatherers do as much as that. And if you greet only your brothers, what is there extraordinary about that? Even the heathen do as much. There must be no limit to your goodness, as your heavenly Father's goodness knows no bounds." (Matthew 5:46-48)

Make a list of the community actions, organizations or movements in which you have been involved, in which people had different faiths, beliefs or ideologies than yours. Were you all struggling for justice, for human rights? What methods did you use? Was political action necessary?

List the difficulties you had in deciding your common purpose, strategies and methods to reach your goals and objectives.

List the advantages to working with such a pluralistic group.

1. "Controversial Issues Provide Opportunity to Find God's Will" by Gilbert H. Caldwell. Article in *United Methodist Reporter,* New York Conference, September 15, 1978, p. 2.

Was your faith compromised in those actions? Describe your feelings.

Did you discover anything about your faith in those actions? Did your faith strengthen your participation? Describe.

Should your local church be involved in community actions, organizations or movements in which people have different faiths, beliefs or ideologies? What would be the advantages? Disadvantages?

"Few nations openly oppose the ideals of human rights, yet over the past two decades much more attention has been given to the splinter in the eye of the other than to the log in one's own..." (to quote from the Introduction to Section III). Dwain Epps suggests that the action is at home, right in our own churches, in our own communities. But we can support each other in our common struggles. We can learn from each other. Once again, as noted in Chapter 9, we can profit from the resolutions of the Christian Council of Bombay, as they developed some clear strategies for their local churches:

INTRODUCTION: Numerous experiments in the life and mission of the church tell us that this is a time of transition for the local church. Now our task is to forge new symbols, images, constructs and models that will enable the local church to move from maintenance to mission, from self-serving to self-giving, from static religion to dynamic faith which takes risks, makes mistakes, absorbs novelties and finds its life by losing it. Consequently three basic strategies are proposed.

First, the primary, symbolic activity of the church is seen through its CONTINUING SACRAMENTAL WITNESS. For the furthering of Justice and Peace it is proposed that the worship life of the church, its property and its authority be used to symbolize afresh its intercessory role on behalf of the world.

The secondary strategy is AWAKENING SOCIAL PASSION. Perhaps in the past the compound wall was necessary. But now a new relationship to society has to emerge that acknowledges that the church and Christians are very much "in" the world and that the welfare of the Christian community is found in the welfare of the whole society. Thus an awakening of social passion is necessary to enable the church to play its historic role as the midwife of civilizations. A new approach to Christian education is needed to provide adequate local church study programmes, to train neighbourhood leadership and to coordinate information and research. Both of these strategies are directed toward recreating the context, climate and structures of the local church, permitting a contemporary articulation of the meaning of the love of God and neighbour.

The third strategy is CREATING NECESSARY SIGNS. It is proposed that concrete sociological signs be created. These signs would function as prophetic guideposts and be a visible representation of what is possible for direct action which transcends communal loyalties. This would entail the establishment of concern groups in the local church, the accomplishment of concrete deeds within the churches' neighbourhood, and a mass convention giving momentum to the cause of Justice and Peace.

CONCLUSION: Thus, the proposed strategies of CONTINUING SACRAMENTAL WITNESS, AWAKENING SOCIAL PASSION and CREATING NECESSARY SIGNS enable the local church to recreate its internal life so that it may become aware, trained, and demonstrate its mission to God for the sake of the world.

Our task is clear. If we believe that "Human Rights pertain to individuals and to the human collectives of which they are a part"—if we believe that "the struggle for the defense and promotion of human rights involves recourse to political action"—and if we believe that "Universal human rights apply to our own situation as well as to others": then can we enable our local churches to:

a. Learn to interpret the signs of the times?
b. Agree to be part of the struggles?
c. Understand the need for solidarity?

If so, what would you feel should be the strategies for your local church? What can we learn from the Christian Council of Bombay? Divide your study group into small groups representing a variety of local churches (urban, rural, rich, poor, etc.) and develop strategies.

Additional Resources

A new and very important resource part of this study on Human Rights that you should not overlook is the cassette Sounds in Struggle: Experiences in Human Rights. Produced by Friendship Press and available from either Friendship Press or your denominational supplier for $3.50, this 30-minute cassette dramatically tells the stories of 5 persons who have worked for change in human rights. The cassette is accompanied by a process book with excellent suggestions for incorporating the use of the cassette with this book. Here is a brief "key" for linking the cassette with use in this process book.

• Chapter 3 on "Torture"—use the interview with Dianna Houstoun Page
• Chapter 6 on "A Charter for Racial Justice..."—use the interview with Rhodes Gxoyiya
• Chapter 8 on "To Secure a Correction of Abuses"—use the interview with Marva Watkins
• Chapter 11 on "To Transform Systems Dealing with Conflicts and Crime"—use the interview with Gary Lee Hawes
• Chapter 12 on "Ensure Availability of Food For All"—use the interview with Frances Moore Lappe.

To Set at Liberty Those Who Are Oppressed by Elliott Wright (New York: Friendship Press, 1973).

Steeple People and the World: Planning for Mission Through the Church by John Killinger (New York: Friendship Press, 1977).

People and Systems. A study exploring four countries—U.S., China, Cuba, Tanzania—dealing with education, health care, religion, work, the role and status of women (New York: Friendship Press, 1976).

Making a Difference by Paul M. Dietterich. A process guide for dealing with crisis issues in Justice, Liberation and Development (New York: Friendship Press, 1973).

You Can Be Set Free by Roy Sano. Designed to help readers become conscious of the sources of oppression in society. Graded Press, The United Methodist Publishing House, 201 Eighth Avenue South, Nashville, Tennessee 32202. 1977. 85¢ per copy.

On Being Human Religiously: James Luther Adams by Max L. Stackhouse (Boston: Beacon Press, 1976). These are essays written by James Luther Adams, professor emeritus of Harvard Divinity School.

Jesus and Freedom by Sebastian Kappen. Presents a theology of liberation born out of the author's own situation, in his own country, India. Orbis Books, Maryknoll, New York 10545. 1977. $3.95 per copy.

Theology for a Nomad Church by Hugo Assmann. A Brazilian theologian searches what the Gospel can mean in a world scarred by hunger, illiteracy, and political repression. Orbis Books, Maryknoll, New York 10545. 1976.

Covenants Action Guide and *Human Rights Action Guide*, available from the Coalition for a New Foreign and Military Policy, 120 Maryland Avenue, N.E., Washington D.C. 20002. Single copies 10¢ each; orders of 50-500, 7¢ each.

Human Rights/Human Needs: An Unfinished Agenda, available from the Office of International Justice and Peace, United States Catholic Conference, 1312 Massachusetts Avenue, N.W., Washington, D.C. 20005. 75¢ per copy.

Human Rights Perspectives, a monthly bulletin containing news and reflections on human rights issues around the world is published by the Division of Overseas Ministries, National Council of Churches /USA, 475 Riverside Drive, New York, New York 10027. This bulletin is available free of charge.

Reports on Human Rights, 1977 and 1978 by the Committee on Human Rights, Canadian Council of Churches, 40 St. Clair Avenue, E. Toronto, Ontario M4T 1M9.

Human Relations and other official material on human rights are published by Ontario Human Rights Commission (Provincial Gov't), 400 University Avenue, Toronto, Ontario M7A 1T7.

Issue, a newspaper dealing with human rights in global perspective. Available from Research and Resource in Social Issues, Division of Mission in Canada, 85 St. Clair Avenue, E., Toronto.

A Human Rights Resource Kit is available from the Center for Justice, 2278 Main Street, Buffalo, New York 14214. This kit is filled with articles, audiovisual aids, educational manuals and a human rights notebook. The cost is $30.

Mission Magazine, December 1978 issue featuring Human Rights issues. Published by the Division of Communications (CEMS), United Church of Canada. Order from CANEC Publishing and Supply House, 47 Coldwater Road, Don Mills, Ontario M3B 1Y9. $3.00 for 20 issues.

"The Captive" — A documentary which portrays an American family becoming a captive of poverty. Set in Appalachia, but pertinent to every locale, the film traces the inevitable direction of a man of dignity who cannot find work. 28 minutes. Black & white. Sale: $150; write for rental information. CC Films, Room 860, 475 Riverside Drive, New York, New York 10027.

"The Jail" — A documentary, filmed in San Francisco, showing the constraints of a county jail system through interviews with prisoners and their jailers. Their personalities and frustrations are exposed, as is the lifestyle in an American prison. 81 minutes. Black & white. Rental: $85 if no admission charges; $150 if admission. Cinema 5, 595 Madison Avenue, New York, New York 10022.

"Last Chance for the Navajo" — What happens when traditional grazing rights of the Navajo people come into conflict with their own needs to better themselves economically through strip-mining and other energy production? This documentary depicts this conflict along with the attitude of the energy-production company, and efforts of the tribe to resolve it. 30 minutes. Write for rental and sale information. CC Films, Room 860, 475 Riverside Drive, New York, New York 10027.

"Life and Death: Dawson, Georgia" — A videotape story of the case of the "Dawson Five": five very young Black men who were accused of armed robbery and murder of a white customer during the course of holding-up a small grocery store. The tape portrays the "Five" as prisoners of a system of racism and poverty. Since the tape was made, overwhelming evidence presented at the pretrial hearings proved their innocence. Write for rental and sale information. Public Television Library, 475 L'Enfant Plaza, S.W., Washington, D.C. 20024.

"Broken Treaty at Battle Mountain" — Documentary about the Western Shoshone Indians of Nevada and their struggle to retain their culture and their land. Opens up the whole issue of the rights of Native Americans to their land. Narrated by Robert Redford. 59 minutes. Distributed by Tricontinental Film Center, 333 Avenue of the Americas, New York, N.Y. 10014.

"Attica"—Investigation of the 1971 Attica prison rebellion which ended in a massacre. Includes interviews with inmates, Commissioner Oswald, families, and footage from the McKay Commission. Looks broadly at prisons, justice, and the treatment of people in America. 80 minutes. Tricontinental Film Center, 333 Avenue of the Americas, New York, N.Y. 10014.

"Collision Course"—Interviews with involved members of the Catholic Church and the Marcos government in the Philippines. An economic picture of the country is presented, showing the working class people and their poverty. Political repression is reported on. An overview of the "real" situation in the Philippines. 40 minutes. No fee; cost of shipping. Justice and Peace Office, Maryknoll Fathers, Maryknoll, New York 10545.

"The Church in Korea—Anno Domini"—Political and social conditions of South Korea in the mid-seventies. The major thrust is the case of eight political prisoners who were part of a student group, the People's Revolutionary Party, who were executed. Some mention of U.S. involvement with the Park government. 40 minutes. No fee, cost of shipping. Justice and Peace Office, Maryknoll Fathers, Maryknoll, New York 10545.

"A Sense of Loss"—Marcel Ophuls' documentary interviewing Protestants and Catholics, government officials and ordinary people, caught up in the Northern Ireland conflict. Their in-depth discussions not only show the hatred that exists, but also the compassion of a people who are tired of having to worry about the safety of their children regardless of what side they are on. 135 minutes. Rental: $100 if no admission charged; $200 with admission. Cinema 5,

595 Madison Avenue, New York, N.Y. 10022.

"Companero"—The story of the famous folk singer Victor Jara, who was killed in Chile during the military takeover. His wife, Joan, narrates much of the film while her husband's songs are played in the background. A look at the power of the military coup as seen through the eyes of a well-known singer. 60 minutes. Rental: $75; sale: $795. New Yorker Films, 43 West 61st Street, New York, New York 10023.

"When the People Awake"—An introduction to the social transformation which took place when Allende became President of Chile. Includes background, development, and forebodings of impending tragedy, and portrays the contending political forces of the time. 60 minutes. Tricontinental Film Center, 333 Avenue of the Americas, New York, New York 10014.

"To the People of the World"—A report on the conditions of human rights in Chile. Most of the film is two interviews with Laura Allende, sister of President Allende, and Carmen Castille, a militant of the Revolutionary Movement. Concentrates on the far-left aspect of Chilean politics. Film clips show demonstrations and turmoil during the coup. 21 minutes. Rental: $30; sale: $350. Latin American Film Project, P.O. Box 315, Franklin Lakes, NJ 07447.

"Sterilization Among Puerto Rican Women"—How sterilization abuse affects Third World women, shown by examining the specific case of sterilization of Puerto Rican women. Includes interviews with women who were sterilized in New York City hospitals and in clinics in Puerto Rico, discussion of sterilization operations and the manifestations of abuse, and some of the efforts to end abuse. 30 minutes. Latin America Film Project, P.O. Box 315, Franklin Lakes, New Jersey 07417.

"Forward Together"—A documentary about the roots of the Jamaican people, the history of their struggles and the society's evolution. It particularly points out the policies of Michael Manley's government (which won power in 1972) in order to modify the economic, social, and political structures of Jamaica. 58 minutes. Latin American Film Project, P.O. Box 315, Franklin Lakes, New Jersey 07417.

"The Politics of Torture"—This powerful documentary underscores the realities of President Carter's far-from-absolute human rights policy and the shortcomings of Congressional actions, using as examples the Philippines, Chile and Iran, all allies of the United States with long records of human rights abuses. 55 minutes. Available from California Newsreel, 630 Natoma St., San Francisco, CA, 94103.

If Christ
    Had   lept from the cross
    Had
Recalled the blood
                 that
                 striped
                    His
                       face
      the blood
      that colored
      the head
Of each
    Prove-Thyself
      driven
        nail

      If
      He
Had   uprooted that tree

From Golgotha then

    Had   hurled   it at men

They might have believed
He was   as He said
God's Son

And He would not have been.

—Sandra Ruth Duguid

*This poem is reprinted from *Adam Among the Television Trees*, ©
1971 by Word Incorporated. By permission here of Sandra Ruth
Duguid.